THE SPONTANEOUS
EXPANSION OF THE CHURCH

By the same author

Missionary Methods: St Paul's or Ours?

companion volume to
The Spontaneous Expansion of the Church

The Ministry of the Spirit

Selected writings of Roland Allen
With a Memoir by Alexander McLeish
Edited by David Paton

Missionary Principles

THE SPONTANEOUS EXPANSION
OF THE CHURCH
AND THE CAUSES WHICH HINDER IT

ROLAND ALLEN

WM. B. EERDMANS PUBLISHING COMPANY
GRAND RAPIDS, MICHIGAN

PHOTOLITHOPRINTED BY EERDMANS PRINTING COMPANY
GRAND RAPIDS, MICHIGAN, UNITED STATES OF AMERICA

Foreword

R OLAND ALLEN was an Anglican missionary in China from 1895 to 1903. For a few years afterwards he was in charge of an English parish. For the next forty years he was writing on missionary principles. Much of what he wrote seemed to be forgotten. The present work, and an earlier volume, *Missionary Methods: St. Paul's or Ours?*, are the only two that have been regularly reprinted. Allen himself told his son that his writings would come into their own about the year 1960. In fact that year saw the republication in a single volume of many of his other writings (*The Ministry of the Spirit*). But his voice has not been silent during all these years. Quietly but insistently it has continued to challenge the accepted assumptions of churches and missions, and slowly but steadily the number of those who found themselves compelled to listen has increased.

I too have been compelled, reluctantly, and I have watched others being likewise compelled. But it can only be what Allen intended if it is the compulsion of the Spirit. The very heart and life of his message was that the mission of the Church is the work of the Spirit. I have known in my own experience the long years of wrestling with these issues which were needed before a Church was willing to put some of Allen's ideas to the test. But those years of wrestling were not mere 'preliminaries'; they were not an unfortunate necessity arising from the slowness and dullness of committees and clerics. They were part of the essential thing that Allen was concerned about — the re-submission in each generation of the traditions of men to the Word and Spirit of God. On the other hand I have heard of mission boards which decided to 'apply' Allen's methods, and proceeded to issue instructions to 'the field' accordingly. The result could only be disaster. There are no 'methods' here which will 'work' if they are 'applied.' There is a summons to everyone who will hear to submit inherited patterns of Church life to the searching scrutiny of the Spirit.

I think that another word of caution is also in order. Allen was a missionary of the Society for the Propagation of the Gospel. He was a priest of the Church of England nurtured in the Catholic understanding of churchmanship. He was a High Churchman. His ideas about the centrality of the Spirit in missions brought him into fellowship with men of very different kinds of churchmanship. One of them has written of their work together as follows: "Allen's ecclesiastical outlook hardly came into our discussions. We were not interested in the ministry and the sacraments in the way that he was; he joined us in a deep concern for the place and pre-eminence of the Holy Spirit in all the work of the Church everywhere, and in the practical activities that this conviction involved." These words illuminate much of what has happened to Allen's message in these intervening years. Of too many of his interpreters it must be said that they were "not interested in the ministry and the sacraments in the way that he was." In Allen's thought — so far as I understand it — the central place given to the work of the Spirit in no way implies a lessening of the importance of the ordered life of the Church as one divine society bound together in a single visible fellowship with the Lord and His apostles, and visibly united in the sacramental life. If he does not speak much of this, it is because he takes it for granted and seeks to gain a hearing for the aspects of the Spirit's work which have been too much neglected in the tradition in which he was nurtured. To forget this and to read what he says about the work of the Spirit through the spectacles of a tradition which gives little place to order, ministry, and sacrament, can only lead to an atomising of the Church which Allen would certainly have repudiated.

I have thought it right to enter these two words of caution, because the reader should be warned that he is embarking on a serious undertaking. Once he has started reading Allen, he will be compelled to go on. He will find that this quiet voice has a strange relevance and immediacy to the problems of the Church in our day. And I shall be surprised if he does not find before long that many of his accustomed ideas are being questioned by a voice more searching than the word of man.

LESSLIE NEWBIGIN (Bishop)

Foreword

It is only gradually that Roland Allen's *Spontaneous Expansion of the Church* has established its reputation among those who are concerned with the mission of the Church. This is odd since it is in many ways both a more mature work than *Missionary Methods: St Paul's or Ours?* and also more relevant to the particular tasks with which churches and missions have to wrestle today. Nevertheless, the fact that a new edition is called for at the present juncture is, perhaps, a recognition that the book contains much that needs to be said and read just now.

It is over thirty years since it was first written. Yet to read it in 1960 is to appreciate anew the touch of the prophetic with which Allen again and again enlivens his analysis and treatment. Some of the things he says seem commonplace today, but they were hardly talked about in any serious way at the time when he first set himself to produce this book. Many examples could be quoted. He bids us beware, for example, of the growth of nationalism, pointing out that it may make the position of any foreigner difficult. He points the same lesson when he deals with the organization of the Church itself and asks how long the Christians of the land will tolerate the foreign missionary as the guardian of their spiritualities. Allen saw all these things as conditions which ought to be met and faced before they became acute; now that they are obvious all can see them, but not all are ready to say what should be done about them, for they are largely out of our control. Allen had a theory of missions and of the development of the Church which enabled him to face this kind of probable future without misgivings. One wonders—indeed it would be fascinating to know—what he would have to say about such a major transformation as the Communist régime in China.

It is because he combined both insight and foresight, and not only perceived tendencies but was able to lay his finger on their meaning, that his work retains a lasting validity, and can be studied and re-studied with profit. Indeed the *Spontaneous Expansion* is a work which *ought* to be studied more than once since it is a challenge to all our

v

complacencies and all our easy assumptions. Nor is this quality of fresh penetrative criticism, constructive withal, in any material way diminished because in many respects events have overtaken him. And not all of his misgivings have been fulfilled: no less than any of us was he free from the possibility of being mistaken.

It is instructive to turn to Chapter 6 on 'Civilization and Enlightenment', remembering that he wrote it in the 'twenties, when the West had no misgivings about the sacred trust of universal progress committed peculiarly to its hands. In this chapter Allen begs us not to confuse faith in Christ with intellectual and moral advance or even Christian social doctrine. We are, no doubt, less likely to fall into that confusion than were the men of that day. We have been chastened by a second world war, by the rise and spread of Communism, by the vivid realization that we have created instruments of power and horror which we may hardly be able to control; and humbled to find that our popular institutions in Europe, or America, by no means infallibly supply a conviction and purpose sufficient of themselves to endow our civilization with a sense of vision and mission. Thus chastened, we discover that our real mission has all the time been to proclaim the Gospel of the crucified and risen Lord Jesus Christ. Allen was saying this and pleading with us to see it, but it was hidden from our eyes. Few, reading this chapter today, would find much to quarrel with in it; and, indeed, it is better to be wise after the event than not to be wise at all.

Therefore, it is not difficult to see why there should be a renewed interest in Allen's writings. For churches and missions are being forced by circumstances to face the arguments which Allen so ably deployed nearly half a century ago. He himself used to say that fifty years would pass before his views would win wide assent and influence policy and practice.

The modern reader may well find his style repetitive, and sometimes even tedious. But who can blame Allen? In spite of previous editions, it is still only the few who have heeded his teaching. It is in order that this book may continue to be studied, and may attract many new readers, that the World Dominion Press has caused it to be reprinted in a completely new form.

At the same time, it is important to remember that Allen, no less than any other author, must be read with discrimination and judgment, and in some passages with reservations. They are not skilful framers of policies who swallow any man's views wholesale and give them what might be termed an almost mechanical interpretation, in a world where issues—spiritual, political, moral and economic— are intertwined with the utmost delicacy and complexity.

It is when Allen deals with the missionary organizations of the West, as they are, that I find him most difficult to follow. He admits that we have to grapple with the modern mission board or society in its vast range of activity and complex arrangements, as the main agent, hitherto, of 'missionary work'. He is exceedingly pessimistic about the probability of the work of these missions resulting in what he would recognize as self-propagating, self-supporting and self-governing churches. He shows us how to start again from the beginning, but he is not always so clear about how to start from halfway down the course, which is just where most of us have to start from. And I think that here his glances into the future are somewhat misleading, for it seems to me fairly evident that the work of missions, with all their faults, is leading, and has led, to the existence of churches having the marks of true churches of Christ and keen to expand by evangelism.

By common and willing consent the era of missionary domination in the Church has gone and it is no longer possible for the missionary to dominate the Church; it has always been undesirable. It is, indeed, true that the leadership of the churches is often in the hands of men who are only too obviously influenced deeply by the standards and outlooks of the West and are thus not always representative of the indigenous potentialities of their own countries. But when all is said, and much can be said in this discussion, the missions of the West have perhaps managed their affairs in these difficult decades with greater flair and, may one say, with more of the guidance of God the Holy Spirit, than Allen might be ready to admit?

For it is always to be recalled, and emphatically at this stage of history, that there is nothing particularly sacrosanct about what is national or indigenous as such. There are natural and very cogent reasons, many of them of a simple and practical rather than a theological order, why the Church should be deeply rooted in the life, culture and modes of expression of a nation; why it should draw its financial support from its own members; and why it should govern itself, subject to the order of the New Testament, after its own instinct and light. But the true nature of the Church is supranational and ecumenical. Its very existence is a rebuke to the over-weening pretensions of exaggerated nationalism whether in East or West. It should be the glory, rather than the reluctance, of a church to enter into relations of mutual aid with other churches, without reference to nationality as a finally determining factor. It is the function of the missionary society or board once again to be a pioneer and to find out just what this means in personal service, prayer, the supply of means, the exchange of views, and the ordering and value of technical services; or the teaching of, and training in, the faith. But the significance of Allen's present volume lies partly in this, that those who have thoroughly grasped his equal emphasis on each of the three leading words of his own title, the *Spontaneous Expansion* of the *Church*, will most sensitively fulfil the pioneer task of the Church.

The reader should not be put off because Allen uses the term 'native', or refers somewhat indiscriminately to non-Christian cultures and religions as 'heathen'. Few in his time questioned the propriety of such terms. Similarly, the 'mission field' was the correct description of the scope of the mission of his day. That there have been great changes in the relationship between churches and missions is unquestioned, and is, indeed, a response to the truth of Allen's thesis. That there is still a cogent contemporary need to take seriously his thought, and, in doing so, not to be deterred by the defects of his sometimes peculiar style and punctuation, seems to be equally certain.

KENNETH G. GRUBB

December 1960

Contents

CHAPTER I

Introduction to 1927 Edition

I

M any years ago my experience in China taught me that if our object was to establish in that country a church which might spread over the six provinces which then formed the diocese of North China, that object could only be attained if the first Christians who were converted by our labours understood clearly that they could by themselves, without any further assistance from us, not only convert their neighbours, but establish churches. That meant that the very first groups of converts must be so fully equipped with all spiritual authority that they could multiply themselves without any *necessary* reference to us: that, though, while we were there, they might regard us as helpful advisers, yet our removal should not at all mutilate the completeness of the church, or deprive it of anything necessary for its unlimited expansion. Only in such a way did it seem to me to be possible for churches to grow rapidly and securely over wide areas; for I saw that a single foreign bishop could not establish the church throughout the six provinces, over which he was nominally set, by founding mission stations governed by superintending missionaries, even if he had an unlimited supply of men and money at his command. The restraint of ordination to a few natives specially trained by us, and dependent for their own maintenance and the maintenance of their families upon salaries provided either by us or by the small native Christian community, and the absolute denial of any native episcopate at the beginning, seemed to me to render any wide expansion of the church impossible, and to suggest at the very beginning that there was something essentially foreign about the church which demanded the direction of a foreign governor.

The years that have passed since that early experience, and an examination of our missionary work in other lands, have tended more and more to confirm that impression. I find that many of our missionaries are inclining to take the same view, and that the enunciation of it is often welcomed. Many are beginning to perceive that we cannot establish a foreign church governed and directed by foreigners, and then at some moment say: 'Let us make it indigenous or native by process of devolution.' If the church is to be indigenous it must spring up in the soil from the very first seeds planted. One or two little groups of Christians organized as churches, with their bishops and priests, could spread all over an empire. They would be obviously and without question native churches. But if we establish missions rather than churches, two evil consequences, which we now see in greater or less degree everywhere, sterility and antagonism, inevitably arise.

If the first groups of native Christians are not fully equipped to multiply themselves without the assistance of a foreign bishop, they must wait upon him, and progress will depend upon his power to open new stations, or to provide superintending missionaries. That way lies sterility. If the first groups of native Christians are not fully organized churches which can multiply themselves, but must wait upon a foreign bishop to move, they are in bondage. For years, perhaps for generations, they must accept this bondage; indeed neither they nor their foreign leaders may feel it; but sooner or later they must awake and then I do not see how they can fail to feel resentment. If I were an Indian, or a Chinese, or an African, I should resent most bitterly the attempt to establish the Faith in my country by men who took it for granted that they must control and direct our spiritual life and progress. I should resent most bitterly the domination of foreign bishops and superintending missionaries. I should say:

> They taught us that orders are essential to the church, they taught us that bishops are necessary for the administration of orders, but they insisted that a bishop must be a dignitary with a large stipend, and they insisted that we were not sufficiently educated to be bishops. At rare intervals they ordained some of us, but they never put us into a position to consecrate our own bishops. Thus they kept all spiritual authority in their own hands. Why should all spiritual authority be vested in them? They cannot claim that they are following the apostles in this: they cannot claim that they are obeying a command of Christ. They are simply in bondage to their own traditions; for they must know that we cannot advance without bishops of our own.

However noble they were in character, however considerate in action, however gentle in manner, I should still feel this. No church councils would satisfy me; nothing but a native episcopate, nothing but spiritual authority for unlimited advance would satisfy me. Consequently I am not surprised when I hear that nearly everywhere in our missions there is springing up a feeling of discontent at our domination; for I myself, who am neither Indian, nor a Chinese, nor an African, feel it to be wrong.

The equipment of small native congregations of Christians with full power and authority as local churches would remove most, if not all, of the present causes of trouble. We should cease to talk of a native church as something to be attained after long years, or generations of probation. There would be native churches at once which all men would recognize as native. There would be ample opportunity for the ablest and strongest native minds to exercise all their powers in the direction and advancement of the churches. Without further words we should have proved to all men that we do not preach Christ in order to extend our dominion as our enemies assert: we should have proved that we really mean the words which we now too often use without any demonstration that we really know their meaning—that we desire to be helpers, not lords over other men's souls.

II

It is scarcely possible to make any statement about our missions which someone will not be found to contradict. Statements of fact are constantly made, and repeated again and again in our missionary magazines, without any question being raised, so long as the conclusion implied or expressed is that men should subscribe more liberally to meet present urgent needs in the familiar way; but if they are used to raise a question concerning the wisdom of our missionary policy or practice, they are disputed. Consequently it has been a question of some difficulty to decide how far it is necessary to support my statements of fact by references or quotations. To have added references and quotations in support of every statement made would have been tedious and absurdly lengthy. I have taken the proverbially risky middle course, and quoted at what may appear to some unnecessary length on points which seemed to me of great importance, as for instance in my treatment of the subject of the training of a native ministry, whilst for matters of less importance in my eyes, or on points which critical and observant readers can find scattered freely in missionary magazines, I have contented myself with a single reference or with none at all.

There is another difficulty which besets anyone who would write of missionary methods in general terms: it is not easy for him to find any expressions which are universally true, or any rules which have no exception. The result is that the moment he makes any statement some individual arises to cry out that that statement is not true, because in his experience it is not true in his district; and thus an impression is produced that the statement in question is a gross exaggeration and that the author is a careless manufacturer of hasty generalizations. Sometimes this charge is made in ignorance of the facts even in that particular district. I remember a man of wide experience telling me that he discussed with a certain missionary the sense of grievance at their subordinate position felt by native mission workers. The missionary answered him: 'Thank God we have not that difficulty here,' yet the first native whom he met when he left the missionary's house began at once to pour forth that complaint. I think that in regard to my earlier books I have been fortunate in that I have suffered much less than I expected from this sort of criticism, but I have not escaped, and could not possibly have escaped from it wholly, and I cannot hope to escape from it now. I can only ask my readers to believe that I have not written anything carelessly; I can only ask them to remember that the district with which they are familiar is not the only district in the world; I can only ask them to pay heed rather to the essential principles than to the particular details; remembering that a crop of fruit does not all ripen on one day, and that if they did not see the ripe fruit in their district it may be because it has not yet come to its hour. The seed which produced the fruit may be there, and it is into the character of the seed which they are sowing that I ask men to inquire, that they may not be taken by surprise when the fruit appears.

A very able and distinguished missionary who kindly read this book in manuscript objected that I talked too much of 'tendencies'. He said: 'You are always saying that something *tends* to produce something else.' That is exactly what I mean. I try to point out that certain seed must produce certain fruit, and I illustrate by saying that the fruit from that seed has appeared in this place or in that. That surely is what I ought to do, if it is my object, as it is, to persuade, as far as I can, my readers to avoid planting one kind of seed and to plant another in its stead.

III

I ought perhaps to say one word on the plan of this book. I begin by trying to set forth the nature of the force which issues in spontaneous expansion and the dangers of checking it. Then I point to some hesitating attempts in modern days to recognize and give place to it. Then I set out the difficulties which hinder us from giving place to it, the terrible fears which beset us, fears for our doctrine, our moral standards, our ideas of civilized Christianity, our organization. In doing this I argue that such fears are real and natural but wicked, that the standards which we so highly prize are not our Gospel, and that the attempt to maintain them by our control is a false method.

Spontaneous expansion must be free: it cannot be under our control; and consequently it is utterly vain to say, as I constantly hear men say, that we desire to see spontaneous expansion, and yet must maintain our control. If we want to see spontaneous expansion we must establish native churches free from our control. I would ask my reader to keep ever in mind this fundamental truth, and to remember that when I speak of churches I am not thinking of pseudo-national churches, national only in name, but of local churches, like those founded by St Paul, churches fully established with their proper ministers. If my reader does not bear this in mind, I fear that he will utterly misinterpret all those chapters which deal with doctrine and morals and organization and read them as though I was dealing with these questions in themselves. It is only in relation to the spontaneous expansion of the Church that they have any place in my argument. Finally I attempt to suggest a way of escape from our present position.

CHAPTER 2

The Nature and Character of Spontaneous Expression

I

When we turn from the restless entreaties and exhortations which fill the pages of our modern missionary magazines to the pages of the New Testament, we are astonished at the change in the atmosphere. St Paul does not repeatedly exhort his churches to subscribe money for the propagation of the Faith, he is far more concerned to explain to them what the Faith is, and how they ought to practise it and to keep it. The same is true of St Peter and St John, and of all the apostolic writers. They do not seem to feel any necessity to repeat the great Commission, and to urge that it is the duty of their converts to make disciples of all the nations. What we read in the New Testament is no anxious appeal to Christians to spread the Gospel, but a note here and there which suggests how the Gospel was being spread abroad: 'the churches were established in the Faith, and increased in number daily',[1] 'in every place your faith to Godward is spread abroad so that we need not to speak anything';[2] or as a result of a persecution: 'They that were scattered abroad went everywhere preaching the Word'[3].

This was not a peculiar note of the apostolic age, a sign of the amazing inspiration and power of apostolic preaching and example: for centuries the Christian Church continued to expand by its own inherent grace, and threw up an unceasing supply of missionaries without any direct exhortation.

Nor was the result of the preaching of these unknown missionaries the creation of a multitude of detached groups of believers in cities and villages all over the Empire. All these groups were fully equipped churches. The first knowledge that we have of the existence of

[1] Acts 16. 3.
[2] I Thes. 1. 8.
[3] Acts 8. 4.

6

Christians in multitudes of places is the name of their bishop in the list of those attending some council. There was order in the expansion: the moment converts were made in any place ministers were appointed from among themselves, presbyter bishops, or bishops, who in turn could organize and bring into the unity of the visible Church any new group of Christians in their neighbourhood.

Thus it came to pass that:

> Seventy years after the foundation of the very first Gentile Christian church in Syrian Antioch, Pliny wrote in the strongest terms about the spread of Christianity throughout remote Bithynia, a spread which in his view already threatened the stability of other cults throughout the province. Seventy years later still, the Paschal Controversy reveals the existence of a Christian federation of churches, stretching from Lyons to Edessa, with its headquarters situated in Rome. Seventy years later again, the emperor Decius declared that he would sooner have a rival emperor in Rome than a Christian bishop. And ere another seventy years had passed the cross was sewn upon the Roman colours.[1]

This then is what I mean by spontaneous expansion. I mean the expansion which follows the unexhorted and unorganized activity of individual members of the Church explaining to others the Gospel which they have found for themselves; I mean the expansion which follows the irresistible attraction of the Christian Church for men who see its ordered life, and are drawn to it by desire to discover the secret of a life which they instinctively desire to share; I mean also the expansion of the Church by the addition of new churches.

I know not how it may appear to others, but to me this unexhorted, unorganized, spontaneous expansion has a charm far beyond that of our modern highly organized missions. I delight to think that a Christian travelling on his business, or fleeing from persecution, could preach Christ, and a church spring up as the result of his preaching, without his work being advertised through the streets of Antioch or Alexandria as the heading of an appeal to Christian men to subscribe funds to establish a school, or as the text of an exhortation to the church of his native city to send a mission, without which new converts deprived of guidance must inevitably lapse. I suspect, however, that I am not alone in this strange preference, and that many others read their Bibles and find there with relief a welcome escape from our material appeals for funds, and from our

---

[1] Harnack, *Mission and Expansion*, ii, 486.

methods of moving heaven and earth to make a proselyte.

But men say that such relief can only be for dreamers, that the age of that simple expansion has gone by, that we must live in our own age, and that in our age such spontaneous expansion is not to be expected; that an elaborate and highly organized society must employ elaborate and highly organized methods, and that it is vain now to sigh for a simplicity which while it existed had many faults and infirmities, and, however attractive, can never be ours. I must, of course, admit that, if that saying is true, if it is really better that paid missionaries should be sent out by an elaborately organized office, and be supported by a department, and directed by a head-quarters staff, if it is really true that our elaborate machinery is a great improvement on ancient practice, and that to carry the knowledge of Christ throughout the world it is in fact far more efficient than the simpler methods of the apostolic age, then indeed I must acknowledge that to sigh after an inefficient simplicity is vain, and worse than vain. But if we, toiling under the burden of our organizations, sigh for that spontaneous freedom of expanding life, it is because we see in it something divine, something in its very nature profoundly efficient, something which we would gladly recover, something which the elaboration of our modern machinery obscures and deadens and kills.

We must not exaggerate the efficiency of our modern highly organized missions. In the year 1924–25 when a force of 1,233 foreign missionaries, aided by 15,183 paid native helpers, and supported by 603,169 baptized Christians, was under the direction of the most highly organized of our Missionary Societies (the Church Missionary Society), the number of adults baptized in the year amounted to 31,329; that is 1.9 to each paid worker, on the assumption that the 603,000 baptized Christians did nothing at all to spread the Gospel. That is no doubt efficient as we count efficient work; but it surely leaves something to be desired.

In Madagascar for twenty-five years all missionaries were driven from the island and a severe persecution of the Christians was instituted. 'Yet,' we are told, 'at the close of a quarter of a century of persecution the followers of Christ had multiplied ten-fold.'[1] Later the missionaries were allowed to return. Mr Hawkins describes the period (1870–95) as a period of great development:

[1] *I.R.M.*, Oct. 1920, pp. 573, 574.

The staff of all the missions at work in the island was greatly increased, churches were erected all over the central province of Imerina, the work was extended to other parts of the island, hundreds of schools were established, and a theological college founded for the training of the native ministry. Handsome memorial churches were erected in Tananarive on the sites where the Christian martyrs had yielded up their lives. A normal school and high schools for boys and girls were started, a medical mission was established, the organization of the native church perfected.[1]

But did the followers of Christ multiply ten-fold in these twenty-five years or in the twenty-five years which followed this organization? That we are not told.

II

If we seek for the cause which produces rapid expansion when a new faith seizes hold of men who feel able and free to propagate it spontaneously of their own initiative, we find its roots in a certain natural instinct. This instinct is admirably expressed in a saying of Archytas of Tarentum quoted by Cicero:

> If a man ascended to Heaven and saw the beautiful nature of the world and of the stars his feeling of wonder, in itself most delightful, would lose its sweetness if he had not someone to whom he could tell it.[2]

This is the instinctive force which drives men even at the risk of life itself to impart to others a new-found joy: that is why it is proverbially difficult to keep a secret. It is not surprising then that when Christians are scattered and feel solitary this craving for fellowship should demand an outlet, especially when the hope of the Gospel and the experience of its power is something new and wonderful. But in Christians there is more than this natural instinct. The Spirit of Christ is a Spirit who longs for, and strives after, the salvation of the souls of men, and that Spirit dwells in them. That Spirit converts the natural instinct into a longing for the conversion of others which is indeed divine in its source and character.

III

Where this instinct for expression, this divine desire for the salvation of others has free course, there it exercises a most extraordinary

[1] *I.R.M.*, Oct. 1920, pp. 573, 574.
[2] *De amicitia*, xxiii, 88.

power. That power is vividly suggested by M. Taine in his *History of English Literature*. Speaking of the causes which led to the Reformation in England, he describes the way in which knowledge of 'salvation' spread through the country:

> Seul à seul, quand il est sûr de son voisin il lui en parle, et quand un paysan parle de telle sorte à un paysan, un ouvrier à un ouvrier, vous savez quel est l'effet.[1]

Spontaneous expansion begins with the individual effort of the individual Christian to assist his fellow, when common experience, common difficulties, common toil have first brought the two together. It is this equality and community of experience which makes the one deliver his message in terms which the other can understand, and makes the hearer approach the subject with sympathy and confidence—with sympathy because the common experience makes approach easy and natural, with confidence, because the one is accustomed to understand what the other says and expects to understand him now.

What carries conviction is the manifest disinterestedness of the speaker. He speaks from his heart because he is too eager to be able to refrain from speaking. His subject has gripped him. He speaks of what he knows, and knows by experience. The truth which he imparts is his own truth. He knows its force. He is speaking almost as much to relieve his own mind as to convert his hearer, and yet he is as eager to convert his hearer as to relieve his own mind; for his mind can only be relieved by sharing his new truth, and his truth is not shared until another has received it. This his hearer realizes. Inevitably he is moved by it. Before he has experienced the truth himself he has shared the speaker's experience.

To all this is added the mysterious power of a secret. Christian experience is always a secret; and the man who speaks of it to another always pays him a subtle compliment when he entrusts him with his secret of life. But when, as is often the case in the mission field, that secret is a dangerous secret; when careless speech may lead to punishment, disgrace or persecution when the speaker entrusts his hearer with the safety of his life, or his liberty, or his property; such confidence, such trust, compel attention.

Upon the speaker, too, the effort to express his truth exercises a profound effect. The expression of his experience intensifies it; it

[1] Bk. II, Ch. v, p. 310, 3rd Edition, 1873.

renews it; it repeats it; it enlightens it. In speaking of it he goes through it again; in setting it before another he sets it before himself in a new light. He gets a deeper sense of its reality and power and meaning. In speaking of it he pledges himself to the conduct and life which it involves. He proclaims himself bound by it, and every time that his speech produces an effect upon another, that effect reacts upon himself, making his hold upon his truth surer and stronger.

But this only if his speech is voluntary and spontaneous. If he is a paid agent both speaker and hearer are affected by that fact. The speaker knows, and knows that the other knows, that he is employed by a mission to speak. He is not delivering his own message because he cannot help it. He is not speaking of Christ because Christ alone impels him. Do men not ask our paid agents: 'How much are you paid for this work?' And must they not answer? And does not the answer destroy the effect of which we have been thinking?

One of the great virtues of spontaneous voluntary expression is that, in the effort to express to another a truth which the speaker has found, he not only renews the past, but, especially in the early stages, he finds out his own ignorance of many aspects of his truth, and he is generally eager to learn, and to inquire further for himself. He searches diligently for answers to difficulties which arise. He is not an authorized and licensed preacher; he has no professional omniscience to maintain; he can and will confess ignorance and seek help. He is forced to think over and over again what are the implications of his truth; he has few ready-made stereotyped answers. As he goes on, no doubt, these tend to multiply, but they cannot multiply at first without much real experience. Thus the voluntary spontaneous expression of truth experienced strengthens and advances the speaker.

IV

Nevertheless, we instinctively distrust it. 'You know,' says M. Taine, addressing his readers, 'you know the effect of such speech as that.' We do know it; but most of us know it rather by an effort of the imagination than by experience. If M. Taine had appealed to us and said: 'You know the results,' would not most of us have answered with no less confidence, 'We do', and would not our minds have turned at once to the rise of those curious and dangerous Anabaptist and Antinomian sects whose wild vagaries exercised the wisdom and patience of sober, sensible men in their own day, and our own curiosity and wonder. When M. Taine says: 'You know the effect,' we think of men like John Bunyan. If he had said: 'You know the result,' we might have thought of that widespread knowledge of the Bible, of that sober, serious temper, of that grave and orderly conduct, which put an indelible stamp for good on the character of our nation; but we instinctively thought first of heresies, schisms, party railings and disputings, the wild licence of individual inter-pretation. If that is true, it is but an illustration of our modern attitude towards spontaneous expansion. It raises at once the question whether it is in its very nature desirable; and the instinctive thought in our minds has condemned it beforehand as an irrational method of religious progress. It is clear that while it possesses all those advantages of which I have spoken, it also opens the door for the unbalanced manifestations of a wild enthusiasm; and we, today, certainly incline to dwell upon the latter rather than the former. That fact by itself alone, is sufficient to explain its comparative absence in our missions.

We fear it because we feel that it is something that we cannot control. And that is true. We can neither induce nor control spon-taneous expansion whether we look on it as the work of the individual or of the Church, simply because it is spontaneous. 'The wind bloweth where it listeth,' said Christ, and spontaneous activity is a movement of the Spirit in the individual and in the Church, and we cannot control the Spirit.

Given spontaneous zeal we can direct it by instruction. Aquila could teach Apollos the way of God more perfectly. But teaching is not control. Teaching can be refused; control cannot be refused, if it is control; teaching leads to enlargement, control to restriction. To attempt to control spontaneous zeal is therefore to attempt to restrict it; and he who restricts a thing is glad of a little but does not welcome much. Thus, many of our missionaries welcome spontaneous zeal, provided there is not too much of it for their restrictions, just as an engineer laying out the course of a river is glad of some water to fill his channels, but does not want a flood which may sweep away his embankments. Such missionaries pray for the wind of the Spirit but not for a rushing mighty wind. I am writing because I believe in a rushing mighty wind, and desire its presence at all costs to our restrictions. But if that is what we are talking about, it is futile to imagine that we can control it. Let us begin by acknowledging that we cannot. If we do that, we may escape from the confusion created by those who say that they have spontaneous expansion in their missions and welcome it and rejoice in it; and yet say also that they are sent to control and must control.

By spontaneous expansion I mean something which we cannot control. And if we cannot control it, we ought, as I think, to rejoice that we cannot control it. For if we cannot control it, it is because it is too great, not because it is too small for us. The great things of God are beyond our control. Therein lies a vast hope. Spontaneous expansion could fill the continents with the knowledge of Christ: our control cannot reach as far as that. We constantly bewail our limitations: open doors unentered; doors closed to us as foreign missionaries; fields white to the harvest which we cannot reap. Spontaneous expansion could enter open doors, force closed ones, and reap those white fields. Our control cannot: it can only appeal pitifully for more men to maintain control.

There is always something terrifying in the feeling that we are letting loose a force which we cannot control; and when we think of spontaneous expansion in this way, instinctively we begin to be afraid. Whether we consider our doctrine, or our civilization, or our morals, or our organization, in relation to a spontaneous expansion of the Church, we are seized with terror, terror lest spontaneous expansion should lead to disorder. We are quite ready to talk of self-supporting, self-extending and self-governing churches in the abstract as ideals; but the moment that we think of ourselves as establishing self-supporting, self-governing churches in the Biblical sense we are met by this fear, a terrible, deadly fear. Suppose they really were self-supporting, and depended no longer on our support, where should we be? Suppose self-extension were really self-extension, and we could not control it, what would happen? Suppose they were really self-governing, how would they govern? We instinctively think of something which we cannot control as tending to disorder.

v

That we in our missions see comparatively few signs of a force so mighty and so universal is in itself a sufficient proof that there must be in our method of work some strong restraining influence. That we so often ascribe absence of missionary zeal to the incapacity of our converts rather than to that restraining influence is a sufficient proof of our blindness. That we at once pray for manifestations of zeal on the part of our converts, and instinctively shrink from steps which may tend to realize it is rather sad than surprising. The force is indeed so strong as to be alarming.

This instinct which makes for spontaneous expression is so powerful as to be alarming, but it is not in its nature opposed to order. It is essentially a social instinct. Islam, we are told, spread in Africa mainly through the spontaneous activity of its converts; but that expansion is not disorderly, in the sense that it is opposed to Islamic order. It does not break the Muslims into innumerable sects; it does not cast away the orthodox Islamic teaching, it does not prefer disorder and disunion.

If the natural instinct is not opposed to order, still less is the Divine Spirit opposed to order. Yet both may be driven into opposition to established order. When the desire to express that natural instinct, that God-given grace, finds itself confined by the order of a superior authority, or by the conditions set up by authority, it is so strong that it can with difficulty be restrained. If men feel that they are acting in any sense against the will, implied, or expressed, of authority, they burst all bounds, and then there is danger of the wildest excesses; for they begin by breaking down the only order v.hich they know, and in bursting away from that which would restrain them they express themselves in violent hostility. Yet they desire order. How little the spirit which creates spontaneous expansion is naturally opposed to order may be seen in the history of the Reformation in England. Then men received a doctrine of 'salvation' which gave them new hope, and they could not refrain from propagating it; but they were opposed by the religious authority of their day. Then at the risk of life they persisted in expressing this instinct to share a joy, this grace which seeks the salvation of others. They broke away from all the order which they knew, and wild excesses were the immediate result. Yet even so, though the movement was in opposition to the ordered religious life of the country, the wildest excesses were confined to comparatively few, and the great majority desired order, and in a remarkably short space of time created order, even in schism.

But perhaps it may be said that what we fear is not the free expression of this natural instinct, still less of this divine grace; what we fear is the expression of human self-will and self-assertion. These are the real sources of disorder; and unhappily men are not moved solely by the pure zeal of the Gospel. We cannot possibly open the door to an unrestricted freedom for the expression of the natural instinct and the spiritual grace without opening it also to the expression of self-will; and that we dare not do.

That is quite true; but unhappily it is also true that we cannot check the licence of self-will without checking at the same time the zeal which springs from the natural instinct and the grace of the Gospel. We cannot distinguish the activity of the one from the activity of the other. The motives which influence the action of human beings are very mixed. Anyone who has tried to analyse his motives for any single action must be conscious of it. Those who exercise authority are not free from mixed motives any more than those who submit to, or resist, the authority. We cannot, then, root up the tares without rooting up the wheat with them. The same action which represses an exhibition of self-will represses also an exhibition of godly zeal. Indeed godly zeal can generally be restrained with a far lighter curb than self-assertion. An exercise of authority sufficiently strong to hold self-will within bounds is often sufficiently strong to suppress zeal altogether.

If new converts once receive the impression that they should express the natural instinct to impart a new-found joy, the divine desire for the salvation of others, only under direction, they are in bonds, cramped and shackled. The zeal dies away, and the Church is robbed of the inspiration which comes from the sense that men are being converted and the Church enlarged no one knows quite how or by whom. The Church is robbed, not knowing how it is robbed; but slowly there grows up a dim sense that all is not well with it, that there has been some restraining influence, and sooner or later the Christians turn upon their directors and accuse them of having in some way held them back. They do not know what is wrong. Zeal for the conversion of their neighbours is not in their hearts or in their thoughts. But it is the suppression of that first zeal which was never expressed which is the real cause of their trouble.

VI

The same truth applies to churches. Spontaneous expansion begins with individual expression, it proceeds to corporate expression, and if the corporate expression is checked there is again a danger of disorder. The denial of a native episcopate, the denial of self-government, seems at the moment to be a great security for order, and for the moment it is; but it represses the instinct for self-propagation and mars the fullness of life. For the instinct must then be stifled. That it should be stifled is a grievous loss to the whole body, for it means stagnation, and the stagnation of a part is a source of poison to the whole. The momentary security is thus gained at a serious cost, and it can only be momentary. The instinct for expression is so strong that it cannot long be restrained. Then must be repeated on a larger scale the struggle which we saw in the case of the individual. The time which this process may take to come to a head is perhaps longer than in the former case, but the longer the time the more serious is the upheaval. Here, too, it is not the desire for expression which produces the disorder, it is the desire breaking out against order because it cannot express itself within the order which it knows. That, too, is grievous; it means the rending of the body; and that is a sore evil and a source of evil to the whole body. The only alternative is that it should have free course within the order of the whole.

VII

Neither the natural instinct, nor the grace of the Gospel, nor the self-will of man can be permanently eradicated by any external authority. Self-will is the natural enemy of order; godly zeal is its natural ally. Restraint forces godly zeal into opposition to order: sooner or later it must break forth and, if it breaks forth in opposition to order, self-will and self-assertion appear as its allies and flaunt themselves in the guise of the deliverers of godly zeal. It is dangerous to restrain what cannot be permanently crushed: *Naturam expellas furca tamen usque recurret.* We are in far greater danger of serious disorder when, in fear of the expression of self-will, we restrain a God-given instinct, than when we accept the risks involved in giving it free play. Yet because we can for the moment by an exercise of authority, or by our influence, or by the influence of the conditions which we create, or by an insistence upon Law, avoid the obvious present dangers of freedom, we naturally tend to think this the safer course.

VIII

It is said that when God announced to the Angels His purpose to

16

create man in His own image Lucifer, who was not yet fallen from heaven, cried: 'Surely He will not give them power to disobey Him.' And the Son answered him: 'Power to fall is power to rise.' Lucifer knew neither power to rise, nor power to fall, but that word 'power to fall' sunk deep into his heart, and he began to desire to know that power, and he plotted from that day forward the fall of man. He fell himself, and he taught man to know his power and to use his power to fall. When in the fullness of time he saw the redemption wrought by Christ, he began dimly to understand that power to fall is power to rise; but he understood it crookedly. Hence, as Christ's disciples began to multiply, and his own kingdom to be minished, his mind turned instinctively again to this power to fall. If he could check, or hinder, the power to fall, he might also, he thought, check the power to rise. He began by trying to induce the apostles to bind all the Gentile converts within the hedge of the Mosaic law, and he was foiled by the boldness of the faith of the great Apostle of the Gentiles. But ever since he has sought to attain his end, striving to induce the servants of Christ to deprive new converts of the power to fall, by hedging them round with laws of one kind or another, in the hope that so he might deprive them of the power to rise: and men, knowing the terrors of falling, and dreading the power to fall for new converts, are only too ready to listen to him; for he plays upon their fears.

CHAPTER 3

Modern Movements Towards Liberty

It is, I suppose, now almost universally admitted that we cannot hope, by multiplication of missionaries, to reach the vast populations of China, India and Africa, not to mention the rest of the world, nor to cover the whole of these great areas with mission stations, still less to provide mission schools and hospitals sufficient to supply their needs. The demands made upon us by our present missions for money and support tend rather to increase than to diminish from year to year. Dr Arthur Judson Brown has pointed the moral for us. Speaking generally of the work of societies, European and American, he says:

> Some of the most expensive missions in the world today are those which have the largest native churches. Surely there must be an end to this process some time. If we were to admit that the more successful the work of establishing a church the greater is the obligation of the home church to sustain its various needs, it is not difficult to foresee disaster.[1]

Mr G. Hibbert Ware, speaking from the point of view of the missionary in charge, is not less emphatic. He says:

> If the mission is to be expected, not only to gather and train the new congregations, but to keep hold of them, and to control their organization and finance, and to raise up and supervise their clergy, and all this for an undefined period which may run (as it has already in some cases) into fifty years, then one may well ask how long this process can go on; how long the mission will be able to support the growing burden of its congregations.[2]

The limits which bound this method of propagating the Gospel must be comparatively narrow. Thoughtful men have now for some years been urging that we are rapidly coming to the end of our tether, and that we cannot hope to multiply our stations much

---

[1] *I.R.M.*, Oct. 1921, vol. x, p. 481.
[2] *The East and the West*, July 1917, p. 259.

further. If we attempt to satisfy a demand for new missionaries and new stations which increases with every new station which we establish; and if the stations which we at present hold are, as they notoriously are, inadequately staffed; and if we find it difficult, as we undoubtedly do find it difficult, to secure sufficient men and money to maintain our present stations, schools and hospitals; and if we attempt, as we must attempt, to carry the Gospel to the whole world; is it not apparent that the size of the work and the method do not agree? Yet in practice we are still acting as if we could go on multiplying mission stations indefinitely.

Even if the supply of men and funds from Western sources was unlimited and we could cover the whole globe with an army of millions of foreign missionaries and establish stations thickly all over the world, the method would speedily reveal its weakness, as it is already beginning to reveal it. The mere fact that Christianity was propagated by such an army, established in foreign stations all over the world, would inevitably alienate the native populations, who would see in it the growth of the domination of a foreign people. They would see themselves robbed of their religious independence, and would more and more fear the loss of their social independence. Foreigners can never successfully direct the propagation of any faith throughout a whole country. If the faith does not become naturalized and expand among the people by its own vital power, it exercises an alarming and hateful influence, and men fear and shun it as something alien. It is then obvious that no sound missionary policy can be based upon multiplication of missionaries and mission stations. A thousand thousand would not suffice; a dozen might be too many.

Many have realized this, and have argued until it has become an axiom, repeated, if not clearly understood, by all our leaders, that our missionaries must aim at laying such a foundation that India may be evangelized by Indians, China by Chinese, Africa by Africans, each country by its own Christians. That certainly must mean that our missions ought to prepare the way for the evangelization of the country by the free spontaneous activity of our converts, and that their success must be measured not so much by the number of foreign missionaries employed, or by the number of converts, as by the growth of a native church in the power to expand. But when we ask how the way is to be prepared for that free spontaneous activity, we find divergent opinions and no settled policy consistently followed by our missionary societies. Many seem to act as if they believed that it is our duty to carry the Gospel to all the inhabitants of the globe ourselves; many simply employ as many native agents as possible, and call that the evangelization of the country by the natives; most attempt, at the same moment, to follow different and opposite methods, hoping to reap some benefit from each, and utterly unable to make up their minds to pursue any consistent policy. Among those who think seriously about the preparation of converts to evangelize their own countries, two conflicting theories, involving two conflicting methods of missionary work, are widely held, and these demand our careful consideration.

I

On the one hand, there are those who hold that it is our prime duty to establish in each country a church, not necessarily very widespread, nor very numerous, but highly educated, and equipped with all the help that science and art and organization can supply; that we ought to concentrate upon a few even within the church, educate them in the arts of healing and teaching and church government, establish them in our doctrine and ethics, and so prepare them to direct the church in its great missionary work when the time is fully ripe and the church so founded has advanced to such strength that it is not only able to take over all the work which we have begun, but to carry it forward into all the corners of the land.

Those who hold this view, and they are very many, are apt to appeal to the authority of Christ Himself in support of their theory. They say that Christ concentrated on the few, and trained apostles who should afterwards guide and direct His Church in the great missionary enterprise which He set before them; and they urge that, if we would follow His example, we should make it our chief business to train leaders, and to build up the church which they may lead.

Now we cannot but observe that there is a great gulf between the training of leaders by Christ and the training of leaders in the hands of these men. Christ trained His leaders in two or three years; these men have been training leaders for more than two or three generations. Christ trained His leaders by taking them with Him as He went about teaching and healing, doing the work which they, as missionaries, would do; we train in institutions. He trained a very few with whom He was in the closest personal relation; we train many who simply pass through our schools with a view to an examination and an appointment. Christ trained His leaders in the midst of their own people, so that the intimacy of their relation to their own people was not marred and they could move freely among them as one of themselves; we train our leaders in a hothouse, and their intimacy with their own people is so marred that they can never thereafter live as one of them, or share their thought. I have heard of students in theological colleges so ignorant of the religion of their own people that they had to be given lectures on it by their foreign teachers. Thus, whether we consider the length of time devoted to the training, or the number of the leaders trained, or the character of the training, or its manner, or its method, we perceive at once that the training of leaders of which we speak is something utterly different from that which we set up as the example, and to which we appeal as the authority for our practice.

If the end which we have in view is the evangelization of the country, and it is to do that work that we establish the church and train its leaders, then our training should be training in evangelization. But in the theory which I am now examining there is a distinction between the training and the evangelization. The church is to be founded, educated, equipped, established in the doctrine and ethics and organization first; then it is to expand. The insertion of this term between the first evangelization by foreigners and the second evangelization by the native church, introduces a grave danger. In putting the advancement of the church first, we teach the converts and the leaders whom we train, so soon as they arrive at consciousness of the direction in which they are being led, to look upon their own progress as of the first importance, to concentrate upon themselves. But that is not training for the evangelization of the country. Great advance in this direction is compatible with a complete absence of any zeal for the conversion of others; and, indeed, is at times definitely opposed to expansion. For instance, I was told the other day that there was a considerable feeling amongst the younger and more highly trained Christian students in India against the admission into the church of large numbers of illiterate converts from among the outcastes, on the ground that such admission tended to lower the prestige of the Christian Church in India which had, through many years, built up a reputation as a highly educated community.[1]

We need not be surprised at this, for we are quite familiar with the unhappy fact that it is possible for Christian churches to be highly organized and equipped and yet to fail utterly to understand the necessity for carrying the Gospel to the people around them. History is full of examples and warnings. Some utterly perished, some survived, persecuted and tormented, and some degenerated in faith and morals. 'He that saveth his life shall lose it.' That danger hangs close on the heels of a practice which puts the elevation of a young church in the foreground and treats the work of evangelization and expansion as something which must follow.

But it may be said that those missionaries who believe in and practise this theory do not neglect to keep ever in view the evangelization of the whole country as their ultimate object, nor do they neglect to train the native church for that work. They establish missionary societies and boards of missions as part of the organization of the Church, and already these societies and boards have sent out missions into other parts of the country.

To this it must be replied, first, that these societies and boards, being fashioned in a Western model, have been established, and can be established, only after a long period of preparation, during which the native church is being educated; so that, in fact, the term between the first evangelization by the foreign missions and their agents and the second evangelization by the native church remains; and it is in the introduction of that term that the danger to which I have pointed lies. Again, missions thus made a department of church organization hold the same relation to the great mass of the Christians which our foreign missions hold to the great mass of Christians at home: they are foreign missions supported by funds to which the Christians may

[1] 'A hindrance to the self-realization of the Indian Church that some at least of her leaders feel is . . . the downward pull of the mass movements as these pour year by year ignorant multitudes into the Church. The new leaders eager to discover and to express the real spirit of Indian Christianity and to advance under the guidance of that spirit to new and independent achievement, feel themselves held back by this weight, so immobile and inarticulate.'—Dr Nicol MacNicol in *I.R.M.*, Ap. 1920, p. 219.

'There are many Indian Christian leaders of repute who look upon this new movement with alarm, and urge that the missions, far from giving countenance to it should discourage it with all their power.'—Mr Cumaraswamy in *The East and the West*, Oct. 1920, p. 342.

or may not subscribe. They are one department of church organization among many others designed for the equipment of a well constituted church; and they are the one department which could be
weakened, or neglected, or abolished without any immediate and
uncomfortable consequences for those who neglected them. If any
other department, the medical, or the educational, or the church
sustentation department, for instance, were neglected all would
speedily feel the consequences. Thus, this objection that expansion
has its place in the education of the native church *as a department* of
church organization, even where it is really made a department,
does not at all invalidate my argument that the introduction of a
period in which the church concentrates upon its own advancement opens the door for all those dangers which beset the self-
seeking.

When new converts are trained to look forward to a day when the
church of which they are members will attain to such strength that
it will be able to carry on all the work which its foreign teachers
began; when their leaders are trained to do precisely the same kind
of institutional and organizing work which the foreign teachers have
done, there arises a serious danger of conflict; and when, as at the
present day, there is a strong tide of national feeling opposed to
foreign domination, this conflict, which would, in any case, be
inevitable, is quickened and exacerbated. Missionaries often say
that the resentment expressed by the more highly trained and intellectual of our converts against the domination of the foreign
missionary is only a part of the universal national feeling which has
been so marked a feature of the last few years. That is not an adequate explanation. The form of expression is moulded often by the
common national unrest; but the conflict between the missionaries
and the leaders whom they have trained was inevitable, and would
not have failed to appear even if there had been no national
movements; for this conflict arises out of the very nature of the
case.

We are constantly being told that the very object and meaning of
the training of leaders for the church is that they may lead the church
and carry on all those works which the foreigners inaugurated, so
that the foreigners may be able to retire and enter upon fields as yet
untouched. All have been told again and again that such is the
missionary's design. Young men are then trained to lead, and, as

C   23

generation after generation passes by, impatience inevitably grows, and would grow, if there were no national movement to excite it. The longer he stays and the more elaborate his institutional work becomes, the less does the foreign missionary seem prepared to retire to give place to the native leaders whom he has trained. The native students have been trained to lead and they have been trained to express their powers by doing precisely those things which the foreign missionary does; but when they have been trained they find that the foreign missionary cannot trust them to do that work sufficiently well to relinquish it to them, and that only subordinate posts are open to them. It is easy for the foreign missionary to say that only generations of training will produce the character and capacity to direct such great and important undertakings; but these young men see their fellow-countrymen taking the lead in great commercial and political and social movements, and they, not unnaturally, say: If the foreign missionary trains us to lead he ought to entrust us with the position of leaders.

Hence arises an inevitable struggle for the control of church policy and administration in the church councils and for the higher posts in the church and in mission institutions between the missionaries and those whom they have trained; for they have trained them not for a work in which there is unlimited opportunity, but for the tenure of positions of which there is only a limited number. But that the history of the advance of a church should be the history of a struggle between the foreign missionaries and their converts for the dominant position in the church is deplorable. The immediate result is that missionaries find it more and more difficult to attract the more intelligent and capable young men to prepare in our institutions for church work. From all sides we hear the complaint that the ablest men hesitate to put themselves or their children under our training for this purpose. From all sides we hear that, where we have had training institutions longest, there the zeal of the church for the propagation of the Gospel is weakest, there the complaints that we do not give the natives sufficient authority are bitterest, and there the tendency for the church to become self-centred is most marked.

Thus this method must inevitably lead to disaster. In some parts of the world able young men, trained in the way which I have described, are already agitating. In India and in South Africa there are loud threats of revolt, and our leaders already begin to fear schisms of a most serious character.[1] When these mutterings and threatenings become violent, then our missionary statesmen begin to talk of devolution and of nice adjustments of claims, measuring carefully how much they must resign, how much they can still afford to retain in their own hands; but they do not consider that everywhere, where now there is apparently perfect calm and their sway is still undisputed, they are pursuing a method of training which must inevitably lead to the same trouble in years to come, and that they are preparing for their successors difficulties compared with which in magnitude the present difficulties appear like the small dust in the balance. Whilst these missionary statesmen are busy about the nice calculation of more and less, they fail to see that their compromises can never bring peace, and that everywhere they are taking a course of action which can only end in a struggle for power. They imagine fondly that they are quite ready to retire when the leaders whom they train are ready to take their place and that the moment when the native leaders are ready will be so obvious that they will all agree that it has come, and that then there will be no difficulty in handing over authority. The moment is never clear. Those who are seeking to gain authority never agree to wait until those who hold it think that they are sufficiently prepared. The moment arrives only when those who are seeking to gain authority are strong enough to drive those who hold it into concession, by threats of revolt. The inevitable result of this method is discontent and strife.

II

On the other hand there are those who think that as a work should end so it should begin. If the propagation of the Gospel is to be at any time the spontaneous work of native Christians, it should be so from the very beginning. Every moment of delay is a moment of loss, loss for them, loss for their country.

There has certainly been of late years a steady movement in the

[1] 'Many leading natives are pressing all Bantu people to come out of the church of the Europeans and establish a church of Natives with Native rules, Native laws and a God who will hear Native prayers and permit Native customs.'—Bishop W. Gore Browne's letter in *Kimberley and Kuruman Diocesan Magazine*, Oct. 1923, p. 3.

'Before the War the call for real devolution was growing insistent, and in some missions of the Society it was becoming quite clear that the dissatisfaction of the educated Christians at the state of tutelage in which they were kept was becoming very serious.'—Report of CMS Delegation to India, 1921–1922, p. 17.

direction of encouraging, recognizing, and, above all, expecting, great advance to be made in this way. Perhaps because the leaders of missionary societies are more and more inclining to lay stress on concentration and institutional work, and consequently are little by little withdrawing from evangelistic work and starving it, the small force of evangelistic missionaries, seeing their numbers decreasing and their power waning in proportion to that of the workers in institutions, are becoming more and more inclined to look upon the growth of the church in numbers by the spontaneous activity of their converts as the only hope of future evangelistic work; and are being forced by the withdrawal of supplies of men and money from home to look to the supplies of men and money on the spot with new eagerness and understanding. Whatever the cause, a movement in that direction is clear.

Before, however, we consider this movement it is essential that we should examine a formula in which Bishop Tucker of Uganda, following Mr Venn, summed up the object of our missions, as the foundation of self-extending, self-supporting and self-governing churches; because it has exercised a very great influence over the thought of those who are moving in the direction of the establishment of indigenous churches. This formula, popularized by Bishop Tucker, was itself a symptom and a cause of this movement; for Bishop Tucker himself proclaimed it in days when the rapid growth of the church in his diocese lent a peculiar force to his teaching. His formula passed almost into an axiom, so that it is today repeated on all hands as an axiom; whilst yet on two important points its meaning has never been made clear either by him or by his followers. The first of these is the relation of the three terms in his formula to one another: the second is the meaning of the word 'churches'.

(1) We constantly hear men use these three terms, self-support, self-extension and self-government, as if they were distinct and separate things, and we find that men have aimed at one or another of them more or less by itself, as if it could be detached from its fellows. Now I believe that a moment's thought will reveal the fact that they cannot rightly be so treated.

Self-support is universally considered a mere matter of finance. No more striking example of the extraordinary materialsim of our missionary outlook can be found than this, that we can only with definite and painful effort think of self-support in any other terms than that of money. The moment that we hear the word self-support we think at once of money and of money only. But any true self-support is more than financial. However wealthy a church might be, it would not be self-supporting unless it supplied its own clergy as well as its own church buildings. However poor it might be, it would yet be self-supporting if it did produce its own clergy and carry on its own services, though its ministers might receive no salaries, and its services be held under a tree. But the ministry is certainly the key of self-government. Bishops and priests imply government. A church which could and did supply its own ministry must be to a large extent self-governing, or at any rate could be self-governing, for it would have within itself the keys of government and authority. Thus self-support and self-government are closely knit. And as for self-extension, it is surely plain that a church which could neither support itself nor govern itself could not multiply itself. Individuals in it might make converts from outside; but those converts would either be dependent upon the church to which their instructors belonged, or would be without any government at all, mere isolated churchless Christians. If the churches of our foundation are to be self-extending in the sense of self-propagating, they must necessarily possess the power to create their like, and unless they are self-governing and self-supporting they cannot possibly propagate themselves. How can a church with no government of its own create a self-governing church? The formula demands that we should establish self-supporting, self-governing and self-extending churches, and obviously, if it applies at all to us, it applies likewise to the churches which we establish. If we are to establish self-supporting, self-governing and self-extending churches, so certainly must they. If the rule applies to the parents of the first generation of churches it applies to the parents of the second generation, and the third, and so on. Thus self-extension is bound up with self-support and self-government: the three are intimately united.

Whether Bishop Tucker perceived this, or not, is not clear, but it is quite clear that his followers all over the world who quote his formula have not perceived it; for they attempt to seek each of the three terms of the formula separately, at different times, and by different means, and this as we shall see has led to weakness.

(2) Bishop Tucker did not make clear what he meant by 'churches' in his formula.

What are the 'churches' which are to be self-governing, self-supporting, and self-extending? In the New Testament I find such churches: the church at Antioch, the church of the Thessalonians, the church which is at Corinth, the church in somebody's house. I read of the churches of Galatia, the churches of Asia, the churches of Judea. These 'churches' were local groups of Christians fully equipped with ministers and sacraments and were exactly what Bishop Tucker desired the churches of our foundation to be, self-supporting, self-governing and self-extending. But I do not know whether he was thinking of churches like these; for in our day, we more often speak of churches of our foundation in a very different sense. We speak of the Church of Japan (the *Nippon Sei Ko Kwai*), the Church of China (the *Chung Hua Shêng Kung Hui*), the Church of Uganda, the Church of South Africa, the Indian Church, and so forth. These are churches very different from the apostolic churches, and their self-support and self-government and self-extension are very different from the self-support, self-government and self-extension of the churches of St Paul's foundation. They are in character national churches, like the Church of England, and if they ever establish other self-supporting, self-governing and self-extending churches like themselves they must do so in some other country than their own; for in their own country they can only extend by increase in the number of their members and subdivision of dioceses, that is by the lowest form of propagation, propagation by fissure, whilst the churches of St Paul established new self-supporting, self-governing and self-extending churches like themselves in the nearest towns or villages, not by fissure but by spiritual procreation.

They differ also from the apostolic churches in another more important particular. In those churches ministers and sacraments were provided for every little group of Christians: in these of our foundation they are the peculiar property of a few favoured centres, whilst the great majority of the Christians are compelled to live without any resident ministers, and thus their priests are not local and resident officers but mere occasional visitors, and the administration of the sacraments becomes an occasional and rare, instead of the normal and the constant, element in their religious life. So far as the majority of the Christians are concerned their familiar and everyday guides and leaders are young lay catechists and school teachers. These churches then are utterly different in character from the apostolic churches.

Finally, they differ from the churches of the apostolic foundation in that they are largely supported and directed by foreigners. If such churches can be called churches at all it is only by identifying the foreign bishops and missionaries with them; whereas the apostles were never the local pastors and teachers and directors of any of the churches which they founded. They were members of them in virtue of their common membership in the unity of the Church which was composed of all the churches; but they were not members of the local churches viewed as local churches, and did not control the details of their social and religious life as local churches. They had nothing to do with their local finance or church building, or anything of the sort. Those churches were never dependent in any sense upon ministers or money derived from some outside source. Consequently if we make any distinction in our minds (and we can hardly avoid making the distinction) between the native Christians and the foreign missionaries supported by foreign funds and employing foreign funds in their administrative work, we see at once that the native Christians cannot be a self-supporting, self-governing and self-extending church apart from the foreign missionary bishops and their missionary assistants, until they are capable of assuming control of all the manifold and complicated machinery of a great national institution; for though they may be very small in numbers in the midst of a vast heathen population, yet their machinery is designed for great national churches. Consequently, until they can carry it, the missionaries who imported that machinery must bear its expense and burden.

It is true that many missionaries like to do this, but whether it is wise to load a small body of Christians in a heathen country with the cumbrous machinery of a great national church, and whether it is wise to subvert the whole apostolic conception of the Church in order to do this, is perhaps open to question, and I venture to question its wisdom.

If anyone says that the word 'churches' in the formula refers to the little groups of Christians in the towns and villages, and that Bishop Tucker habitually spoke, as his successors do, of these as 'churches'; then all I can say is that St Paul certainly did not found churches without local ministers and sacraments. If the local congregations are in our eyes churches, then we must acknowledge that, since these churches have neither ministers nor sacraments, we are creating a new type of church which has no biblical authority whatsoever, and is not in harmony with our own Prayer Book, which, following the Bible, takes it for granted that local churches have local ministers and sacraments. The Prayer Book certainly does not contemplate churches ministered to by lay catechists and teachers, still less does it contemplate half-a-dozen or a dozen such in the care of a lay cate-chist; yet that is a common thing in the mission field. In the Telugu Country 'a catechist has charge of at least ten or a dozen congre-gations in as many villages'.[1] In February 1924, Bishop Lasbrey told us that there was 'only one clergyman for over a hundred churches'[2] in the Isoko Country on the Niger. In the Church Missionary Society Report for 1923–24 we are told that in Nigeria 'The Rev C. W. F. Jebb, who is in charge of the Owo district, is responsible for no less than 250 churches, including several in the outlying region of Kabba'. And that in Uganda 'One native clergyman is responsible for 185 churches! Another is responsible for 205 churches! There are young teachers responsible for forty, fifty, and sixty churches, and to superintend this great work there are just two European clerical missionaries.' It is impossible for us to call such congregations 'churches' in the biblical sense of the word, unless we are prepared to maintain that the Pauline churches were mere collections of Christians in towns and villages without local presbyters and local observance of the Lord's Supper as their regular common ser-vice.

I am persuaded that this is wrong and that our attempts to found national churches without the substructure of the local church is a mistake. Those little groups of Christians which are sometimes called 'churches' but are not, ought, as I think, to be churches in the biblical sense and ought to be instituted and equipped as the Pauline churches were instituted and equipped, and then the unity of these would represent, and might one day become commonly recognized as, the national church of the country; but to begin with the national church and to build that on a foundation of local groups of Christians which are not churches seems to me a fatal inversion. I believe that we ought to return to the apostolic practice and found churches in

[1] EW, 1915, p. 208.
[2] CMS *Outlook*, Feb. 1924, pp. 27, 28.

every place where we make converts, churches equipped with all the divine grace and authority of Christian churches.

It would appear as if Bishop Tucker had formulated the truth by a kind of inspiration; but that he failed to bring it to the birth because he did not attempt to reconcile the idea of the 'churches' of which he spoke with the idea of the 'churches' from which he borrowed his inspiration. He allowed that word to escape from him unquestioned and undefined, and consequently the church over which he was set as Bishop in Uganda boasts that it is self-supporting whilst it depends (depends in a very real sense) upon large grants from England; boasts that it is self-extending whilst it cannot propagate itself; for though it can multiply Christians it cannot beget churches; boasts that it is self-governing whilst its foreign bishop and his assistants proclaim that it must have the guidance of bishops and superintending missionaries from England for long years to come. If Bishop Tucker had accepted the apostolic idea of 'churches' and had followed the apostolic practice, there might, and would, have been in Uganda hundreds of self-supporting, self-governing and self-extending churches today; whereas now we receive the same kind of appeal from Uganda that we receive from other dioceses abroad which make no boast of being self-supporting or self-governing.

Now we shall find when we examine the modern movement towards spontaneous expansion that this confusion exercises a very disturbing influence. Men constantly use the word 'church' both of the church of the country, and also of any one of these little groups of Christians which have neither local presbyters nor sacraments, as though each was a church in the apostolic sense of the word; whereas, in fact, neither is such.

Confusion here must inevitably lead astray men who desire to see the propagation of the Gospel in any country the spontaneous work of native Christians from the very beginning. So long as we continue to think of the churches which we are to establish as great national churches composed of huge dioceses governed and directed almost exactly as our churches are governed in England, but composed largely of congregations, which are called churches and are not, it is almost impossible to conceive the spontaneous activity of native Christians resulting in the creation of new churches; but the moment that we think of churches in the apostolic sense of the word, we see at once that the spontaneous activity of the individual members of such churches might very speedily result in the multiplication of churches all over the country.

III

We can now consider what movement has been made of late years in this direction.

(1) There is certainly today amongst many of our missionaries a tendency to encourage their converts to teach others from the moment of their conversion. That may seem a very strange thing to say, and it would be a very strange thing to say unless it were still somewhat rare, and was not even now checked and hindered, often by those who desire it most sincerely.

(*a*) *It is hindered by a very widespread conviction amongst our missionaries that new converts, so far from evangelizing others, need to be nursed themselves if they are not to fall away.* We often hear some such expression as this: 'Even after baptism the new life in Christ must be carefully tended or inevitably the first fervour will cool and the early enthusiasm will be quenched by the deadly heathenism all round.'[1] That is a voice with which we are very familiar, which teaches that the way to retain the consciousness of a gift received is not by handing it on to others, but by learning to depend more and more on teachers; and that it is our wisdom to expect nothing from our converts, but to watch over them and nurse them and feed them. It is a voice which appeals more and more insistently for paid and trained workers to guard and to protect a life which must otherwise *inevitably* be quenched.

(*b*) *It is hindered by a very widespread conviction that we cannot trust untrained men to propagate the Faith.* That is openly said by many; by many more it is believed, or half-believed. Even those who encourage their converts to propagate the Faith have doubts in their minds, and hasten to supply teachers to take charge of any work which they find to have been started by the spontaneous zeal of native converts, and they do this even when they know and confess that the teachers whom they send are very inadequately trained, and certainly have not the initial zeal of those whom they are sent to supplant.

That such action must check the spontaneous activity in the future of those who are so treated is obvious. When men are allowed to think that when they have begun to learn, and to practise what they

[1] CMS *Gleaner*, April 1921, p. 72.

have learned, the way of advance is to surrender their activity, they speedily learn the fatal lesson of inactivity; more cautious or timid people, who might have been inspired by their success to imitate their example, are checked, and wait for the trained and paid teacher; whilst inquirers and heathen onlookers learn from their own observation that in the eyes of the missionaries the teaching which the untrained zealous convert gives spontaneously and freely is to be lightly esteemed in comparison with the teaching of the paid native agent.

They all learn this lesson the more readily when they find that it is the proper thing for converts to pay the salary of a Mission agent; because the payment gives his teaching still more importance in their eyes.

(c) *It is hindered also by an action of ours which is designed to support it.* When converts are taught from the very beginning that they receive to hand on, and when they practise this with the inevitable consequence that there is a great advance made, and when this is reported at home, it often results in our being stirred to send them men and money to establish institutions for their intellectual advancement and to supply them with 'better trained' teachers. Now this action, which is designed to encourage them and to help them, seems often to hinder them. They learn to receive, they learn to rely on paid and trained men. The more teachers they have, the less they feel the need for exerting themselves to teach others. That is perhaps quite natural, but it is disastrous.

More serious, however, than any of these is the fact that this personal evangelism can never come to fruition in the establishment of new churches except in that form of 'church' guided by lay catechists or teachers under the supervision of a superintending missionary, which we have already rejected as unapostolic. In early days one of the most powerful causes of the expansion of the Church was the presence of the apostolic churches with their ordered life and spiritual rites in the midst of the surrounding heathenism. That influence is not indeed destroyed, but it is weakened very seriously by the fact that the 'churches' which result from efforts of spontaneous evangelists today are not really native, but dependent upon the care of foreign superintending missionaries. Any graces which the new Christian community shows can be ascribed to the influence of the foreigner and to his direction: they do not spring plainly and unmistakably from some new spirit brought into the life of men who in all respects live exactly as their heathen neighbours except that they use strange religious rites and are somehow subtly different from other men, and do the same things as other men in a different spirit. That witness of the corporate body cannot be clear so long as the government of white men and the control of an imported teacher stand in the foreground. Self-extension by the mere existence of a purely native church is hampered and rendered difficult, because men cannot see it apart from the influence of the foreigners. The evangelistic efforts of the spontaneous evangelist are clear; but he is followed by the paid teacher and the paid cleric and behind all is the white superintendent and the white bishop. They are never forgotten and where they appear the witness of the life of the native church becomes misty and blurred. All progress can be ascribed to their influence, their teaching, their schools, their control. There the spontaneous effort of the native evangelist is marred and the witness of the Christian community which he gathers together is marred. Only when the non-Christian population is face to face with a change in their neighbours, and an ordered church life of their neighbours which can be ascribed to no white influence, are they compelled to face the fact that they are in the presence of a spiritual force which is strange to them, in the presence of the Holy Ghost.

Nevertheless there has been in the last few years very considerable advance, advance so great and in so many different parts of the world that it is making a serious impression upon our minds. If it is true, as it is true, that outcastes in India, and labourers in Nigeria, and Uganda, and China and Korea, are capable, not only of being led and directed to do this work, but of doing it spontaneously of their own initiative, not in one or two rare cases only, but in many, we cannot but be impressed. The same results seem to follow the same teaching all the world over. The conviction that new converts can beget new converts leads them from strength to strength: the conviction that they will fall if they are not nursed leads them from weakness to weakness. The difference lies not in the nature or in the environment of the converts; but in the faith of the missionaries.

(2) Self-support in a strictly financial sense is now one of the popular cries in the missionary world. For a long time men thought it impossible: they declared that the poverty of their converts was so profound that to expect them to provide the material for their com-

mon religious life was absurd, and many of our missionaries still say the same thing today. But that self-support from the very beginning is possible has been abundantly proved, not only in rare sporadic instances, but by the wider experience of those missionaries who set themselves to encourage the evangelization of the country by their converts from the very beginning, and that in spite of the fact that they laid upon them a very heavy and wholly unnecessary burden, by insisting that they must support paid teachers and catechists, and sometimes also clergy, paid at a rate which approved itself to the foreign authorities. In Uganda, when the rapid expansion of the Faith began, the leaders of the movement saw the necessity for ensuring that the new converts should supply what was necessary for their church life, as they understood it, and they made it their boast that in Uganda all native buildings and all native teachers were supported by native funds. And what was proved to be possible in Uganda has been proved to be equally possible in all the other areas where converts have been encouraged to propagate the Faith from the very beginning. This is indeed far from being the same thing as the complete material and spiritual self-support which was without doubt the rule in the church expansion of the early centuries; but it is unquestionably a movement in that direction. And with very beneficent consequences. In Korea 'the self-support method succeeds. Where this principle has been conscientiously followed—there the churches are many and large. . . . Where churches are helped most, there they are weak, lifeless and helpless. This may be easily verified, go where you will throughout Korea.'

This is what we should naturally expect. Nothing is so weakening as the habit of depending upon others for those things which we ought to supply for ourselves. Nothing more undermines the spirit which should express itself in spontaneous activity. How can a man propagate a religion which he cannot support, and which he cannot expect those whom he addresses to be able to support? We ourselves can only propagate a religion which we do not expect our converts to be able to support, because we think that we can supply those necessaries which they are unable to supply. Even we ourselves are beginning to see, as I pointed out earlier in this chapter, that this puts a very strait limit to the extent of our work. Had it been only in consideration of this limit, those who desire to encourage a wide extension of the Church would have been compelled very soon to

35

strive to the uttermost to induce their converts to give as much as possible towards the maintenance of their churches. And this is what we actually see in the case of great numbers of missions which practise a kind of bastard self-support, which is little more than an ill-disguised attempt to wring from the converts as much financial help as possible. The stipendiary system which we have treated almost as if it were divine in its origin makes this inevitable and it issues in sad appeals. 'Since 1922 I persevere to declare, about self-support to every station, to every church, that they ought to offer sixpence everybody, but they cannot do anything. And I fail now; I cannot do anything. I hope my Lord Bishop he will decide this case about self-support.'[1]

Nevertheless, though our steps are hesitating and slow, we are learning a lesson which will one day open the door to true spontaneous expansion. We already begin to see that the Christian Faith is not a way of salvation only for the well-to-do; and that no people are so poor that they cannot maintain all that is necessary to their salvation.

(3) In the matter of self-government we have made the least advance. If missionaries have hesitated to believe in the power of the Spirit of Christ to inspire their converts to preach the Faith which they have found; if they have hesitated to believe that poor native converts could supply the material necessary for their corporate religious life, they have hesitated still more to believe that converts could direct their own religious organization. Even those who have proved by experience that new converts can, and will, from the very beginning propagate the Faith, supply their own church buildings, and even support financially their teachers, hesitate to believe that they can, and ought to, direct their church organization from the very beginning.

Take a case like this:

A few days ago I had a letter from the African pastor who was in charge of a part of the district during the absence of the superintendent. While making a tour in the Akoko Country, a deputation from a village that I had never heard of came to beg him to pay them a visit, saying that their membership was now about 600. 'I went there,' he says, 'and found their statement true.' They had been gathered in by a number of young fellows who had gone down the country to work, and had come in touch with Church Missionary Society workers, had been converted and baptized,

[1] *Nyasaland Diocesan Chronicle*, April 1925, p. 16.

and then returned to found a church in their own village, and to teach all that they had learned. What splendid zeal! What a glorious opportunity! The pastor has appointed as a teacher a young fellow who had lived with me and learned something with a view to becoming a teacher. He is a convert himself, very young, and poorly equipped; we have set him a hard task. The arrangement is not ideal, but is the best we can do.[1]

Now here it will be at once observed that the little group had organized itself and could maintain itself.

Its members met for mutual comfort and support; they combined to provide themselves with such things as were necessary: they were directing all their own organized religious life, until the day that they invited the visit of that foreign trained pastor. Here was self-government from the very beginning. If only that self-government had not been destroyed by the foreign missionary, but had been regularized by the bishop, if their leaders had been ordained, there is no reason in the nature of the case why they should not have continued as they had begun. Then we should have seen true spontaneous expansion issuing in the creation of a new church, self-supporting, self-governing, and, in all probability, self-extending; for this treatment of the first pioneers would certainly have encouraged their converts to follow their example.

But what did the superintending missionary and his African pastor do when they met a case like that? They immediately sent as a teacher to those people a man who is described as 'very young and poorly equipped'. Now why did the missionary superintendent hasten to send a very young and poorly equipped teacher to a place where most zealous teachers had taught with such success that they had gathered a congregation of 600 souls? It was not because there were no other openings for him; because in the very same article the missionary told us that:

> Enquirers in most promising cases, turn away from us because of continual disappointment, as the teacher they had waited and begged for never came, and they had no one to guide and support them. Then a Muhammadan came along . . . and drew them to the faith of the false prophet . . . and those who might have been pillars of the village churches have been taught to become the bitterest enemies of the Cross of Christ.

If the man were fit to be employed at all, he might have been sent to one of these. It was not because the new teacher was likely to be

[1] CMS *Gleaner*, Jan. 1921, p. 9.

better than the old; for though he may have had a little more know-ledge of the missionaries' doctrine, he had not the zeal which con-verted 600 men. It was not because by sending him the missionary established the church. He did indeed bind that group to the mission, but he did not establish the church. Were they any better off when another layman was set over them? They were in worse case than they were before.

But their leaders needed help, and felt the need of help, and therefore they invited the pastor to visit them. Well, of course, they needed help and felt the need of help; but were they helped? I venture to doubt it. To have taught those men a little more, that they might have imparted it to the rest, would have been help: to send a very young and poorly equipped teacher to supplant them was not a help but a hindrance. We ought never to send a mission agent to do what men on the spot are already doing spontaneously. If they cry to us for help, as they often do, we should give them help, but help which would support their position and assist their zeal, not supersede them and kill their zeal; help that should strengthen them as leaders, not make them subordinates. To supersede them is disastrous.

I remember once asking a missionary from Western Africa, whether he had ever known natives set out on their own initiative to teach others what they had themselves learnt of Christ, and he told me how a missionary on a journey found in a village a number of men who met together to hear the Bible read and to pray, and that their leader was a native Christian who had learned something at the mission station. I asked him what the missionaries did when they made this discovery. 'They immediately sent a teacher,' he said. Then I asked him what became of the man who had first begun the work. And he answered that he heard no more of him. That is the natural consequence. If the moment that we find anyone doing anything spontaneously we send a paid man to do it for him, we stop his work and we check others from following his example. All men see and learn the lesson that to join the white man's Church it is necessary to induce the white men to send one of his trained teachers. They see and learn the lesson that the spontaneous zeal of native Christians is deficient in some way. It obviously does not satisfy the white man and his paid native pastors: they do not trust it: they do not encourage it. It is better to get a paid teacher however young and poorly equipped than to have the most zealous unpaid volunteer, for the moment that the white man finds out what is going on he will certainly insist on sending one of his paid teachers.

The result is that we kill voluntary spontaneous activity on the part of our converts, that all men believe that the presence of a paid teacher is essential for their admission into the Christian Church and that the progress of the Gospel is limited by the number of paid teachers available. Expansion ceases with the failure of the supply of natives trained by us. If the natives are converted to any other religion than the religion of Christ they can direct their own religious life. The Muslim, for instance, does not nurse his converts nor send them paid teachers. Converts to Islam seek teaching for themselves that they may lead their fellows: they travel sometimes from Nigeria to Cairo to learn. Christian converts are taught to cry feebly for teachers to be sent to them.

But why do we do this? That question I shall attempt to answer in the following chapters. Here all that I need to do is to beg those missionaries who say that they are anxious to see the Church expanding by the spontaneous activity of their converts from the very beginning, to consider what is the inevitable consequence of action like this. The story which I have quoted is not a rare and exceptional one. There is scarcely a country in the world from which we have not heard the like. Everywhere by robbing new converts of that liberty of directing their own religious life which they enjoyed before the mission teacher was sent to them, we produce the impression that, for some reason, their religious life ought to be directed by the white missionaries and their paid agents. But if men believe that the Christian religious organization is one which they cannot direct for themselves, how can they continue to propagate the religion? Their own experience shows them that the spontaneous zeal of men untrained by the foreigners is inadequate; that some half-trained, paid, man can do what spontaneous zeal cannot do, that is, consolidate and establish the church in its relation to the church of the white missionaries.

If the growth of the church depends upon the supervision of foreigners and of natives trained by them, the extent to which it can grow is severely limited. It depends upon the area which the foreign missionaries can cover, and the number of men whom they can train. The moment that limit is reached expansion must cease. And long before that, the sense that men are propagating a system of religion which is so unsuited to those to whom it is preached that they cannot receive it and practise it for themselves, exercises a very severe restraint. We feel it ourselves. Its influence is most baneful. All our missionaries run with their faces turned backward. The moment that any door of opportunity opens before them, they look behind for support. They continually bemoan the fact that their greatest difficulty, their most serious anxiety, their most bitter disappointment, arises from the lack of support from home. They cry for recruits and the recruits fail to appear, and they see the door of opportunity closing. And the whole body of converts learns this lesson that expansion depends upon the supply of trained mission agents; that the religion which they have adopted is one which natives cannot maintain for themselves; that they must have a foreign overseer or a man sent by a foreigner to minister to them. How can spontaneous expansion flourish in an atmosphere like that?

Until we learn that not only self-support in a financial sense, but self-support in a spiritual sense, a sense that implies self-government, must begin from the very beginning, we cannot hope to see that wide propagation of the Gospel which alone could penetrate a continent like Africa, or reach the vast populations of India and China, or cover those wide, sparsely-populated areas where communications are difficult, or find an entrance into those countries or districts where the Government is definitely opposed to Christian propaganda, places into which no white missionary can penetrate and where no mission stations can be founded. For such work the Church must be free—free with a freedom of which we now scarcely dare to dream. Spontaneous zeal leads Christian men to teach others, often in secret, often at the risk of their lives and property; and they must be able, not only to convert, but to organize their converts. They must be certain that no white missionaries, no paid agents of foreign societies, are necessary for the establishment of the church. They must know where to turn for Holy Orders, and they must be sure that Holy Orders will be conferred. Church must beget church, as individual begets individual. Is not that the only way? Or is our way of looking hopelessly into the world and saying, 'This is closed to us,' 'That is unreachable,' 'We have not enough paid workers,' 'We cannot afford to open a new station,' a better way? Could we once persuade ourselves that self-extension, self-support and self-government go hand in hand, and are all equally the rights of converts from the very beginning, we might see such an expansion of Christianity throughout the world as now we little dream of.

The refusal to recognize that self-government is necessary for new converts is threatening to produce most serious consequences. There is that in the Gospel which demands expression and is never satisfied without propagating itself. We have seen again and again in the history of the Church that a Christianity which does not propagate itself languishes, if it does not perish. And this is true of new churches as of old ones. Wherever the spirit of Christ is, there is the Spirit which desires the conversion of the world to Christ. And when men do not find adequate opportunity for its expression, a spirit of discontent and strife enters in.

At the present moment we hear on all sides mutterings of a coming storm. In India, in Africa, in China there are movements which call themselves Christian, movements which certainly could not have existed if our missions had not been there before them, which are definitely anti-European and anti-missionary. Within the circle of those whom we call our members there is grave discontent. If we continue much longer in our present way, it seems to me to be inevitable that, as our converts all over the world advance in education, so this discontent will grow. The result will be a schism of the most profound and far-reaching character.

We must remember that the vast majority of our converts have been, and are being, educated in dependence, and that the vast majority of our missionaries have not advanced even to the point of believing in the desirability of spontaneous expansion from the very beginning. Even those who believe in its desirability are commonly under the impression that they are labouring with all their might to stimulate it, whilst they are practising those very things which hinder it.

I hope that I shall succeed in the following chapters in persuading my readers that the methods which we have generally followed hitherto have sprung into existence as the almost inevitable consequence of our own attitude and training and that in employing them we have unconsciously, and often unwillingly, created an atmosphere in which spontaneous expansion is almost impossible. It is high time that we should definitely face the question whether we will not in the future return to the biblical apostolic practice and by establishing apostolic churches open the doors for that expansion and make it the foundation of our missionary policy; for we are at a turning point in our missionary history, and what is to be the future course of that history will depend upon the attitude which we take up on this question.

CHAPTER 4

Fear for the Doctrine

One of the most serious difficulties in the way of any spontaneous expansion and of the establishment of apostolic churches arises from our fear for our doctrine. I once heard a missionary from Africa say that if we allowed our converts to teach as the Muslims allow their converts to teach, the doctrine might spread like wildfire. 'But,' he added, 'we could not possibly permit that.'

Such a saying might naturally surprise us. We might have expected that a man who went to Africa to propagate the doctrine would welcome with joy the prospect of its spreading like wildfire through the country. And he would assuredly do so unless he was restrained by some powerful influence. Nor is there any doubt what the restraining influence is. It is fear for the doctrine. He is afraid that the doctrine may be misrepresented by the unguided zeal of native Christians to teach others what they have learned. I do not think he is afraid that his converts would wilfully and deliberately misrepresent it: I think that he rather doubts their knowledge of it, and their ability to express it as he thinks that it ought to be expressed.

This fear compels him to say that we cannot possibly permit native Christians to express their spontaneous zeal in teaching others what they have learned, and in so saying he proclaims that we can generally restrain it, and do so. He proclaims also that, if we did not restrain it, spontaneous zeal would in fact spread the knowledge of the doctrine far and wide. He recognizes the presence and the power of such spontaneous zeal. He says that 'we do not allow', 'we could not permit' it to have free course.

I

Now this saying represents the thought of a very large number of our missionaries abroad, and of our people at home. We often hear it said that we must maintain at all costs our standard of doctrine. We cannot possibly allow untrained and uncontrolled natives to propagate Christianity. It is this attitude that the believer in spon-

43

taneous expansion must meet, and it is, therefore, necessary to examine carefully its character.

But before I do that I would beg all those missionaries who protest that they do all in their power to encourage spontaneous activity on the part of their converts, to consider well whether this saying does not in fact represent their real thought, whether they do not in spirit accept the position that we must maintain our standard of doctrine, and that we cannot permit our converts to teach as the Muslims allow their converts to teach. For it is surely obvious that if we hold this theory spontaneous expansion is impossible. We may welcome spontaneous expansion, or we may refuse to permit it; but we cannot do both at once.

(1) The attitude which 'cannot allow', and 'cannot permit', is obviously the attitude of a governor: it is an imperial attitude. *We* must maintain, we say, *we* cannot permit. We, then, are the guardians of the standard, and we must maintain it not only for ourselves but for all who learn to believe on Christ through our preaching. In accepting our message they accept our direction. They are in our charge and we accept the responsibility for them. Unlike St Paul, we are far from disclaiming lordship over their Faith. The standard is ours, and we must maintain it.

(2) The standard to be so maintained must be a fixed standard; but if we were asked where this standard of doctrine is to be found, what should we say? Should we say, In the Catholic Creeds? That is not what we really mean when we talk about maintaining our standard of doctrine. If we are members of the Bible Churchmen's Missionary Society we mean a certain doctrine of inspiration: if we are members of the Anglo-Catholic party we mean what they mean when they speak of Full Catholic Teaching. It is not the Apostle's Creed that we think of when we speak of maintaining our standard of doctrine, but of some interpretation of it, or of some addition to it. And where that standard is to be found we do not know, for we are not all agreed as to the terms of it.

II

On what do we rely for the maintenance of this standard? When we talk of maintaining it we are obviously not relying on its own inherent truth: it is we who are proposing to maintain it, and we are depending clearly upon some power which we possess to maintain it. There

44

is clearly a great difference between 'contending earnestly for the Faith which was once for all delivered unto the saints',[1] and this maintaining of a standard by authority. When we contend earnestly for a Faith, the emphasis is upon the inherent truth of that for which we contend: when we maintain a standard, the emphasis rests upon the exercise of authority.

On what then do we rely for the exercise of this authority? Without doubt we rely upon our prestige; and in no small degree upon our wealth, and our ability to give to the converts all those material advantages which only money can supply, salaries and buildings and education and hospitals and such-like. This is a fact with which every student of missions at home and every man of experience in the mission field is familiar:

> *Cherchez la bourse* will almost always lead one to the seat of real power in mission administration. Even societies which have been most emphatic in the assertion of the theory of the independence of native churches have found in the power of the purse a sure device by which to guard infant churches from lapses or novel experiment.[2]

We often attempt to disguise it, but it is appallingly true:

> It is far from the thought of missionaries and boards to make their money a means of retaining control, but it is as futile in Asia as it is everywhere else to imagine that real independence is compatible with financial dependence.[3]

When we say we must maintain our standard, we certainly mean that it is *our* standard and not *their* standard; that for some reason they have not so accepted it that they will maintain it themselves. If we ask how it comes to pass that they have not so accepted it, the answer generally given is that it has taken us ages to grow up to our present standard, and that it will take our converts generations to grow up to it, and that meanwhile they cannot maintain it for themselves. That answer simply confirms what I said above, that our standard which we maintain is something of our own age and race. It cannot be the Catholic doctrine in the sense that it is the doctrine of all the ages, of the primitive Christians as well as of us who live in this last age.

[1] Jude i. 3.
[2] A Group Study in *IRM*, April 1920, p. 236.
[3] Dr A. J. Brown in *IRM*, Oct. 1921, p. 489.

It is a question which we might well consider whether new Christians must necessarily begin at that point of development at which we happen to stand at the moment when we go to them. It is a question of still more serious importance whether a standard of doctrine can be really maintained by an external authority as a code of laws can be enforced by a conquering government upon a subject people; or whether a standard of doctrine must not essentially be something internal, maintained by people who really do understand and believe it. It does not seem to me that any maintenance of doctrine which does not spring voluntarily from internal convictions can properly be called a maintenance of doctrine at all. If that is so, for us to maintain a standard of doctrine is a kind of contradiction in terms.

How do we attempt to maintain it? First we make the preparation for baptism long and difficult by insisting upon each convert learning what is for very many of them difficult verbal lessons. Multitudes of our converts are totally unfamiliar with the kind of abstract language which the teaching of our doctrine involves, and consequently what seems to us very simple is for them very hard. When they have learned enough to satisfy their teacher that they are ready for Holy Baptism, they may be baptized, but we do not consider that they are therefore qualified to teach others what they have learned. And very often, if not generally, they do not themselves feel able to teach others; for they instinctively recognize that that kind of teaching is difficult, and that they themselves have not grasped it. Consequently they are not expected, and hardly themselves expect, to do more than listen to the teachers.

Then we train the teachers. We take children quite young and give them special training in elementary schools and high schools and theological colleges, so that they can understand our use of abstract terms and can learn at least verbally our doctrinal expressions; and these men we set over the little congregations, knowing well that in the great majority of cases they do not know enough to do more than repeat exactly what they have been taught.

From amongst these teachers we select the men who repeat best and teach best from our point of view, and to these we give further teaching and then ordain them with great confidence that they will teach nothing but what they have learned from us. And these men we put into positions of greater authority, under superintending missionaries, and I have heard them complain, 'We do what we are told; but we do not understand what we are doing'.

In this way we certainly have succeeded in maintaining a standard of doctrine in the sense that in our missions heresy on any considerable scale is practically unknown. But what has been the result of this method of maintaining our standard?

(1) First a terrible sterility. Our converts have not gone astray from the fold; but they have produced nothing. We have taught them to depend upon us, rather than upon Christ, and dependence upon man produces sterility, dependence upon Christ produces spiritual and intellectual fecundity.

(2) We have convinced the heathen as well as our converts that to become a Christian it is necessary to learn the lessons imparted by one of the trained teachers, or better still to receive the instruction of a foreign missionary himself. This obviously tends to restrict advance to the number of paid and trained teachers, and when there is any widespread movement the missionaries are unable to meet the demand. Then, instead of blaming their method, they lay the blame upon their supporters at home, as if they ought to supply teachers for every village in the world.

Listen to this:

> The pressure on the missionary of masses of these outcasts clamouring for teachers and for baptism at times passes all endurance. Several deputations are on your verandah before dawn, waiting to press their claims.
> 'Sahib, we want you to send teachers to our village.'
> 'I am sorry, but I have none to send.'
> 'But, Sahib, we want to learn all about Christianity.'
> 'I know, but it is impossible.'
> 'But, Sahib, we want to become Christians.'
> 'I am very sorry, but you cannot.'
> 'Sahib, cannot we become Christians?'
> 'No, go away, go away.'
> And the missionary drives them from his verandah, angry, indignant with the apathy of the Church that has placed him in such an impossible position.[1]

(3) The Doctrine has been maintained by external authority, but it has hampered the thought of the people, and as the Christians advance and grow in understanding they begin to feel this dimly and to resent it. The result is that in places where our missions have been

---

[1] W. E. S. Holland—The *Indian Outlook*, pp. 210, 221.

long established and where the converts have made great progress in intellectual education, as for instance, in India, there arises an instinctive, unreasoning, revolt.

When I was in India some years ago I was told repeatedly that young educated Indians were saying, 'We will not have your Western Creeds', but that they very seldom had any reasoned objection to them. As far as I could, I made enquiries for myself, and I found this to be true. Young educated Indians said to me, 'We will not have your Western Creeds'. But when I inquired which particular articles in the Creed offended them, the only answer that I got was, 'You have forced them upon us'.

Thus the maintenance of our standard of doctrine by external compulsion seems to proceed through sterility to revolt.

III

(1) In the early Church we find a very different state of affairs. When the Christian Church was first spreading throughout the Roman Empire she certainly maintained a standard of doctrine, and that standard was not imperilled by the spontaneous activity of a multitude of Christians who were certainly not trained theologians. These unknown missionaries taught the doctrine which they had learned, and that teaching was so far adequate that the bishops of the Church did not hesitate to consecrate new converts as bishops for the new churches without giving them any long or special training in theological colleges.

The great heresies in the early Church arose not from the rapid expansion resulting from the work of these unknown teachers; but in those churches which were longest established, and where the Christians were not so busily engaged in converting the heathen round them. The Church of that day was apparently quite fearless of any danger that the influx of large numbers of what we should call illiterate converts might lower the standard of church doctrine. She held the tradition handed down by the apostles, and expected the new converts to grow up into it, to maintain it and to propagate it. And so in fact they did. The danger to the doctrine lay not in these illiterate converts on the outskirts; but at home, in places like Ephesus and Alexandria, amongst the more highly educated and philosophically minded Christians. It was against them that she had to maintain the doctrine.

Now all this suggests quite a different atmosphere from that with which we are familiar. The Church of those ages was afraid of the human speculation of learned men: we are afraid of the ignorance of illiterate men. The Church then maintained the doctrine against men who were consciously innovating: we maintain the doctrine against men who may unconsciously misrepresent the Truth that they have learnt. The Church then maintained the doctrine by her faith in it: we maintain our doctrine by distrusting our converts' capacity to receive it. The Church then maintained her doctrine by thinking it so clear that any one could understand it: we maintain our doctrine by treating it as so complicated that only theologians can understand it. Consequently, the Church then was quite prepared that any man who believed in Christ should teach others what he knew of Him: we are only prepared to allow men whom we have specially trained to teach it. When others, whom we have not specially trained, of their own spontaneous motion do teach others, we hasten to send a trained teacher to take their place. That is, of course, exactly what the early Church did not do, yet it maintained its standard of doctrine.

(2) And here I would recall the fact that in all those sporadic cases of spontaneous teaching with which we are familiar in our own day we never hear of any deliberate corruption of Christian doctrine. When our missionaries discover these cases, they nearly always find that the teaching given is, so far as it goes, true, and is very often surprisingly true and deep. These converts seem to have learned by themselves much that we think can only be taught by us. And what they have learned is very fundamental. And they seem also invariably to show a great readiness to learn more. Now that is not the spirit which breeds heresy. The spirit which breeds heresy is a spirit of pride which is puffed up with an undue sense of its own knowledge and is unwilling to be taught.

IV

The reason why the spontaneous zeal of new converts does not breed that spirit is not hard to find. Such converts are almost invariably men who have had some real religious experience. They have heard something of Christ; they have received some teaching about Him; they have generally learned to repeat the Creed and to read the Bible; they have called upon Christ and been heard; and this has wrought a change in their whole outlook upon life, such a change that they are eager that others should share their experience. Hence they begin to teach others, and to share their experience with others.

Now all religious experience demands doctrine for its proper statement and explanation. If then these men are not well instructed in the Christian doctrine, when they attempt to share their experience with others they feel that there is much in it which they cannot understand. Consequently instruction in Christian doctrine comes to them with an enlightenment and a power which is a joy, and therefore they gladly receive it, because it supplies a felt need of their spiritual experience. In such an atmosphere Christian doctrine is in little danger, for though false or inadequate teaching, if they received such, might prevail for a time, yet the true teaching when it comes must inevitably drive out the false. For the experience is a true experience, and a true experience demands a true doctrine.

It is as the complement of experience that Christian doctrine first took shape. It is notorious that the Christian doctrine of the Trinity, for instance, was formulated through the attempts of the disciples of Christ to explain their experience. Christ appeared, and the apostles experienced His power: the Holy Ghost descended, and the apostles and their immediate followers knew His indwelling; the Christian doctrine of the Trinity arose out of attempts to express that experience.

It is as the complement of experience that the doctrine continues to have reality and meaning. We can remember how Cyprian wrote to Donatus:

> As I, myself, was held in bonds by the innumerable errors of my previous life, from which I did not believe that I could by possibility be delivered, so I was disposed to acquiesce in my clinging vices; and because I despaired of better things, I used to indulge my sins as if they were actually parts of me, and indigenous to me. But after that, by the help of the water of new birth, the stain of former years had been washed away, and a light from above, serene and pure, had been infused into my reconciled heart—after that, by the agency of the Spirit breathed from heaven, a second birth had restored me to a new man; then, in a wondrous manner, doubtful things at once began to assure themselves to me, hidden things to be revealed, dark things to be enlightened, what before had seemed difficult began to suggest a means of accomplishment, what had been thought impossible, to be capable of being achieved.[1]

[1] Cypr. ad Don. C. 4. Ante-Nic. Libr. VIII, p. 3.

Now here is expressed a doctrine of baptismal regeneration, but it is the complement of experience, and as the complement of experience it is expressed with power, and has all the vigour of a new discovery. And so it is always.

As the complement of experience, doctrine renews its youth from age to age; but divorced from experience it is nothing more than the statement of an intellectual theory, and to rest in something which an intellectual process has created is to rest in that which an intellectual process can destroy.

Doctrine, accepted either as an intellectual satisfaction, or as an authoritative pronouncement, divorced from experience, has no power in itself. In the seventeenth century Richard Baxter, and all his readers alike, believed in the doctrine of a fiery hell, a doctrine delivered with all the weight of authority. Listen to his appeal to men to care for the souls of others, 'What if the man die and drop into hell while you are purposing to prevent it!' What doctrine is there conceivable more calculated to stir those who believed it? Yet Baxter complains, 'Alas, how few Christians are there to be found that set themselves with all their might to save souls!' They believed the doctrine, they assented to it, they accepted it, yet they were not moved by it.

It is vain to say that the doctrine was false or falsely stated, and therefore it failed. It failed not because it was false or falsely stated, but because it was mere doctrine divorced from experience. Experience of the power of Christ to deliver from sin and from fear of the punishment due to sin, did then, and does now, induce zeal; and the preaching of that power of Christ is Gospel; but the other by itself is mere doctrine, and, like all doctrine, in itself lifeless.

We see the same thing today. High sacramental doctrine should make men eager, if any doctrine could make men eager, to provide the sacraments for Christians, and to remove all hindrances which prevent men, anywhere, from using them; but we see those who most glorify the sacraments, glorifying them by external adornment and standing most stoutly for those very things which make the administration of them to Christians in out-of-the-way corners of the world impossible.

In the light, then, of the history of the early Church, and of our own experience of sporadic cases of spontaneous teaching, I venture to suggest that the method by which the early Church maintained its standard of doctrine is superior to ours, and that we should be wise to rely upon the free expression by any convert, however illiterate, of his spiritual experience, and to teach our doctrine as the complement of that experience. But that is nothing else than to open wide the door to that spontaneous expansion which the man I quoted at the beginning of this chapter deprecated, saying that we could not permit it.

Nevertheless the fear haunts us that if we allowed our converts, though they might be illiterate men, to teach freely what they had learned, the doctrine might spread like wildfire, and the country might be covered with multitudes of groups of men calling themselves Christians, but really ignorant of the first principles of Christ; and that thus the Church and her doctrine might be swamped, as it were, with a flood of ignorance. That is the fear which causes young educated Indians to protest against the admission of large numbers of outcastes into the Christian Church; that is the fear which causes some of our missionaries to say that we have no right to receive more illiterate converts than we can really teach.

Here we must observe that so far as these young educated Christians are concerned their fear is much more fear for the prestige of the Church, which has established through many years a reputation for having the highest standard of literacy of any religious body in the country, than for the purity of her doctrine. And as far as the missionaries are concerned they are thinking entirely in terms of a theory and method of missions which limits teaching to a comparatively small body of missionaries and their trained native helpers, and of doctrine almost entirely in terms of intellectual education.

Now I have already tried to show that spontaneous expansion proceeds by an expression of experience much more than by a mere intellectual instruction. This witness of experience brings a spiritual enlightenment, and spiritual enlightenment quickens the intellectual faculties, and prepares the mind for intellectual teaching: it also brings a great readiness to receive instruction. Consequently where there is spontaneous expansion there arise not only a multitude of witnesses to Christ's power; but also a host of teachers, not only ready to impart teaching, but to receive it.

This alters the whole complexion of the problem. For in such a case the Church would have to deal not with the few professional teachers whom she could collect and train and pay; but with a host of unpaid men who were already teaching and eager to teach better. Moreover, under such circumstances men learn an immense amount from one another. They have a very quick eye for perceiving those who among them have a truer grasp of the realities of the doctrine; and they both can, and do, obtain help from them in the form which is most useful to them.

I am not denying that where spontaneous expansion was very rapid there might be very large numbers of dangerously ignorant converts; I am not denying that the fear expressed by these men is a reasonable fear; I am only saying that it is exaggerated because their conception of Christian doctrine is too intellectual, and they are familiar only with the teaching of doctrine which restricts it to a small number of teachers trained in a western manner, with the result that they cannot conceive any true advance in the apprehension of doctrine apart from this western intellectual education.

The mere fact that all these men are driven to declare that they would prefer that the spread of the Gospel should be deliberately restricted is enough to give anyone who is familiar with the Bible reason to think that there must be something wrong. In the Bible the preaching of Christ is not so purely intellectual, the apprehension of Christian doctrine is not so purely intellectual.

v

What Christ asks of His disciples is not so much exposition of doctrine about Him as witness to His power. Now witness to His power can be given by the most illiterate if he has had experience of it. It does not require long training for a man to say: 'Whereas I was blind now I see', even though he may be compelled when asked: 'What sayest thou of Him?' to answer: 'I know not.' Such a man was quite prepared to say: 'I believe' and to worship, when told that his Healer was the Son of God. Christ did not require any long training in doctrine when He said to the Demoniac of Gadara: 'Go and tell how great things the Lord hath done for thee, and how He had mercy on thee.'[1]

I remember a missionary in India telling me that most of the converts in his district were brought in by extremely illiterate men. He said: 'The villagers look at them and say, "We know what you were, we can see what you are; what has made the difference?"

[1] St. Mark 5. 19.

These men cannot preach sermons,' he said, 'but they know enough to answer, "Christ", and the result is men are converted to Christ.' I do not remember that he told me that many evil results followed, or that the doctrine suffered from such witness. The truth is that such witness is a preaching of the doctrine, and of the true doctrine. The doctrine is implied in the witness, though it may not be intellectually apprehended. It is a far more true preaching of the doctrine than a long discourse on the Divinity of Christ. Does anyone seriously think that the doctrine would really suffer in the long run, if India or China, or Africa, were flooded from end to end with the teaching of men who knew enough to say: 'I called upon the Lord and He heard me,' 'I appealed to Christ and He saved me from my fear?' Does anyone doubt that in such ground as that true doctrine would flourish very abundantly? It ought to be a cardinal principle with missionaries that anyone who knows enough to be saved by Christ knows enough to tell another how he may be saved.

There is indeed a certain advantage which the illiterate possesses when teaching illiterate men. When the speaker says: 'I sought the Lord and He heard me,' and he was delivered from precisely those things under which his hearer labours, the witness is far more likely to come home to the hearer than when the speaker was delivered from a sin, a danger, or a fear so refined and subtle that the other cannot understand the fear of it at all. I suppose nearly all those who have tried to help other men have realized this difficulty. They have felt that the only thing to do in some cases is to call in, if they can, the assistance of a man who has actually been delivered from that particular vice, or danger, or fear. They realize that, however strangely to their ears that man may express his experience, yet, if only he will express it truly, his experience may do what their experience cannot do, that is, persuade the inquirer that if he, too, calls upon the Lord, he will be delivered.

There is a danger to which men who have had a literary training are liable, which does not seem to attack the illiterate to the same degree. Mental training teaches us to pay much attention to secondary causes, and unless we are very careful we are apt to concentrate our attention upon the secondary causes: whereas the illiterate, knowing very little of secondary causes, often, or even generally, express themselves in terms of the first cause. The temptation to the trained mind is to dwell on the process by which deliverance came and to forget that the deliverance really preceded the process. While the difficulty seemed yet insoluble, I called and He heard; and the witness is: 'I called upon the Lord and He heard me.' But we are tempted to say: 'I was in a difficulty, and then I thought, and then I saw, and then I argued, and then I heard, and then I put two and two together, and then I found the solution of my difficulty.' It may be all quite true; but in stating the deliverance thus, we somehow alter the emphasis, and the statement becomes rather an explanation than a witness to Christ's power. Now, what distinguishes us Christians from other men is that we know the first cause; other men know secondary causes. But when we dwell upon the secondary causes we are likely to obscure rather than to reveal the first cause. And so instead of bearing witness to Christ we present an argument.

And the argument is never a sufficient explanation, and it is sometimes so weak that it can be easily answered. Moreover, if we succeed by this argument in convincing our hearer, we have only succeeded in convincing him by this argument so far as this argument serves. The moment another difficulty arises to which this argument is not applicable, he must either find another argument which will serve, or he is lost. Only if the witness has taught him to seek the Lord that he may be delivered will he be in a position to meet any difficulty that may arise; for when a soul has once found that Christ can deliver, whatever difficulty arises, he has only to pursue the same course, and call upon the Lord, to be delivered. Thus the presentation of secondary causes too often robs Christ of His Glory, and men of His salvation, while witness glorifies Christ, and sets men upon the true path.

The power of this witness is most profound. 'One thing I know, that, whereas I was blind, now I see,' 'I sought the Lord and He heard me,' are arguments for faith in Christ which may be rejected but, cannot be controverted. They appeal to all, to learned and to simple. When men come into the presence of a real deliverance, they marvel; and, if they have a consciousness of need of deliverance for themselves, they covet it. All down the ages it has been the witness to Christ borne by manifest deliverance which has moved and converted men.

Yet we commonly insist that to propagate the doctrine we must have men who can answer the arguments of opponents. No doubt it is well to have men who can do this, but it is far more important to have men who can witness to Christ simply and truly, for true and simple witness is by far the more powerful weapon. A clever argument may silence opponents, but witness converts them: they see in a deliverance something which all their wit does not supply.

VI

Fear for our doctrine has another serious consequence. It leads us to put the doctrine in the wrong place. We must maintain, we say, our standard of doctrine, we cannot allow untrained natives to teach the doctrine. We cannot but notice that in this saying the doctrine is foremost in our thoughts.

We constantly imagine that this is a matter of no importance. We speak as if the Gospel and the doctrine, preaching Christ and preaching Christianity, were identical terms. It is impossible to read a page of a missionary magazine or to speak five words about missions without finding out how habitually we do this. But is it really true? Far from it: Christianity, the doctrine, is a system of thought and practice: preaching Christ, the Gospel, is a revelation of a Person.

There is a difference between the revelation of a Person and the teaching of a system of doctrine and practice; but our use of the words shows that we find it difficult to grasp this and still more difficult to practise it. Is it possible to reveal Christ to those who have never heard His name without setting forth the facts of His Life, His teaching, His works, His character, His Godhead, His atonement, His priesthood, His kingship; the moral, intellectual, and emotional attitude due to Him; the duties to other men which arise from belief in Him; the effects of belief in Him which have been, and must be, revealed in the lives of individuals and nations; or some of these things, or others like them; and is not all this what we understand by Christianity? Is it possible to propagate Christianity without setting forth these same facts of Christ's life, of His nature and work, and of the duties which follow: and is not this the way to reveal Christ? Can a man expound the doctrines of the Incarnation, of Atonement, of Grace, and not reveal Christ? Can a man say one word about Christ, or even utter His name without preaching Christianity?

Yet there is a difference, and we know it; but we know it only within narrow limits. We know that in our Christian experience we come into contact with the Person of Christ: that is indeed for us the

56

fundamental reality of all realities: it is that which distinguishes us from men of every other religion: and we can distinguish between that contact with Christ and apprehension of a doctrine. And we know that it is possible to apprehend a doctrine without that contact with Christ. And we know it is possible for one to teach, and for another to learn the doctrine, without approaching the Person to whom the doctrine refers. So far, I suppose, we can all distinguish.

What we find it difficult to believe is that others can receive Christ and find salvation in Him unless they know, or at least in speech employ, our familiar doctrinal expressions. We know, of course, in some sort, that people whose intellectual understanding of doctrinal expressions is very weak, or immature, or even false, do draw near to Christ and receive His grace. We can see in the Gospel story and in the history of the Church, and in our own experience in our own day, that ignorance of doctrine does not prevent men from being lovers of Christ, and being saved by Him from vice and sin, and danger and fear. It seems indeed almost ridiculous and profane to think that Christ does not save those who call upon Him because they have not the power to grasp an intellectual doctrine about Him. We know that the doctrine of the atonement has been expressed in different ages in very different forms, some of which seem to us untrue and evil; but we know that in all ages men have found atonement in Christ. Nevertheless our doctrine so dominates our minds that we can scarcely believe that men can love Christ and be saved by Him unless they know and use our doctrinal expressions.

Because we find this difficult we inevitably tend to give the teaching of our doctrine the first place in our work, and to make the teaching of the doctrine prior to the revelation of Christ.

Now this produces very serious consequences. When we preach the doctrine, the doctrine occupies the first place in our thought, and is in the foreground of our mind. When we preach Christ, the Person is in the foreground and occupies the first place in our mind. When we speak of preaching Christianity it is the system of doctrine and practice of which we are really thinking: when we speak of preaching Christ we are really thinking of the revelation of Christ. But the Person is greater than the doctrine and far excels it, and consequently, when we speak of preaching Christianity and pass from the thought of Christ to the thought of the doctrine, we pass from the reality itself to the shadow of the reality.

When we fall into this error, we inevitably tend to make the acceptance of the shadow, the doctrine, the system, the aim and object of our work. In doing that we are doing something of which Christ spoke in very severe terms. To make converts to a doctrine is to make proselytes. The proselyte abandons one system of thought and practice for another; and to adopt a new system of thought and practice is not the way of salvation. The Christian convert is a convert not to a system of doctrine but to Christ. It is in Christ that he trusts, not in any system of doctrine or of morals. The difference between the work of the judaizing zealot and the Christian missionary lies here: that the one sought a convert to his doctrine; the other seeks a convert to his Lord. This distinction is most profoundly important; and it is a matter for very grave anxiety that we have of late years heard missionaries speak of making proselytes. When we put doctrine in the first place, we are in danger of falling into exactly that error which Christ condemned.

But missionaries do fall into this error. It is indeed true that among missionaries are to be found those who are most keenly alive to the reality behind the doctrine, and live most consciously and constantly in His presence; but those of us who are most keenly conscious of the reality are the very men who also realize most clearly the danger of allowing the doctrine to take the first place in our thoughts and expression: they, too, are the first to acknowledge how often we do this. The danger is, indeed, insidious. It seems almost impossible to escape from it. We cannot but teach the orthodox doctrine that we know, and the line between teaching the doctrine so that it reveals Christ and teaching the doctrine so that it usurps the place of Christ, is so fine that we are all constantly in danger of allowing the acceptance of our orthodoxy to become the aim and object of our work.

Now when we say that we cannot allow untrained natives to teach the doctrine we are in grave danger of falling into this error; but the untrained native Christian is not so likely to fall into it as the man who has been trained in our theological colleges. For the one thing which he really knows is his experience of Christ, whereas the other has learned so much of the doctrine of his teachers and has given so much attention to it that he is very liable to fall into this error.

VII

But men will say that native Christians will not spontaneously bear witness to Christ as I have suggested, and that we cannot possibly wait for them to do so. My answer is (1) that when we abandon that attitude which is represented by the saying, 'We must maintain our doctrine, we cannot allow untrained natives to teach the doctrine', when we put Christ first and the doctrine in the second place, and open the door for the spontaneous activity of our converts, when we establish churches with full authority, we shall know whether that is true or not; (2) that sporadic instances of spontaneous teaching by unpaid Christians are now so numerous, in spite of our restrictions, that there is very good reason to believe that such activity would be sufficient to carry the knowledge of Christ far and wide; (3) that the very men who say it is impossible to allow untrained natives to teach, by that very argument show that they are persuaded, as the man whose words I quoted at the beginning of this chapter was persuaded, that native Christians would bear witness to Christ if we did not restrain them. We certainly do not hasten to forbid what we really believe to be impossible; (4) that when we ourselves know and feel the impulse of the Holy Spirit driving us to communicate to others the knowledge of Christ it is really a contradiction of our own experience to say that other men who experience the power of Christ and His Holy Spirit will not do what we know Christ and His Holy Spirit must urge them to do.

I said at the beginning that the motive which urges us to restrain untrained teachers is fear. If it is not that besetting sin of Western people, the lust of control and government, it is certainly fear for the purity of the doctrine. Now when we are dealing with the Gospel fear is a very bad master.

CHAPTER 5

The Christian Standard of Morals

If we are afraid that any widespread spontaneous expansion might endanger our system of doctrine, we are not less afraid that it might endanger our standard of morals. We fear lest new converts might tolerate a standard which we could not recognize as Christian. Many men who believe that they desire and encourage spontaneous expansion are certainly not prepared to encourage any expansion which would involve such a risk. They say: 'We must at all costs maintain the Christian standard of morality'; or, 'We cannot possibly tolerate any lowering of the Christian standard of morals.' We often hear our missionaries contrast their work with that of other teachers, especially, perhaps, with that of Muslim teachers, in this respect, saying that those other teachers pay no regard to the moral conditions of those whom they accept as converts, but that we 'make great demands'.

There are two ways of maintaining a standard of morals. We may keep the ideal presented to us in Christ ever before ourselves and our converts, and seek ourselves, and teach them, to follow it, or we may define a standard and treat that definition as a law which must not be departed from. In the first case we set before our converts an infinite advance, in the second a finite rule. In the first case we must trust in the Spirit given to lead them towards that divine standard of morality, in the second we can trust in our powers of control and direction. In the first case we must expect that others may see a different aspect of truth from that which we see, and reveal to us aspects of moral truth which we could not have seen without their aid; in the second we must insist that they learn precisely what we have learnt, as we have learnt it, and do not deviate from it. In the first case we accept a divine standard, both for ourselves and for our converts; in the second we present what seems to us to be a proper standard, a standard which is more or less Christian, as the case may be, a standard which appears to us Christian, but is something short of the standard of Christ.

I

When we speak of maintaining the Christian standard of morals, what we have in our minds is without doubt the second of these two ideals of a standard; and when we speak of making great demands, it is unquestionably the second of these methods of which we are thinking. For the demands are specific demands. When we say that we make great demands, we do not mean that we set a high moral ideal before our converts, but that we demand obedience to definite rules of conduct. Generally speaking, we treat the maintenance of these definite rules of conduct as synonymous with the Christian standard of morality.

But when we ask what is this Christian standard of morals expressed in demands, and where it is to be found formally laid down, as the Muslim standard of morals is said to be laid down in the Koran, we are met at once by the difficulty that there is no certain answer to these questions. It is certainly not in the Bible; for unless we are prepared to accept the Jewish law in its entirety, there is no code of morals laid down in precise commands for Christians in the Bible as a whole, still less in the New Testament. Our demands do not, indeed, make up a complete and consistent body of law binding on all Christians: they are mere fragments.

And these fragments are selected on no Christian principle. The selection is arbitrary. We treat sins of the flesh as matters for the enforcement of law, sins of temper and spirit we do not. Yet in the Gospels, Christ is not represented as observing this distinction. He denounces sins of pride and self-assertion with a severity no less condign than sins of the body; but we do not refuse to admit men who give way habitually to a hot temper, or indulge a supercilious, insolent, haughty and contemptuous manner towards those whom they consider their inferiors. Why? Is it because these sins are in truth less dangerous and immoral than sins of the flesh? Is it certainly true that a man who commits these offences is less guilty before God than a man who, having followed the custom of his tribe, has more than one wife, or even than a man who, following the custom of his tribe, gets drunk at a feast? Is a man who gives way to fits of impatience whenever things do not go to his liking less a sinner because he conforms to our standard of external purity, than a man who can show a most Christ-like patience and meekness under ill-treatment, yet is bound by circumstances to a life which we call a life of sin, a condition from which he cannot escape except by an act of most questionable morality? Why do we act so differently towards these two? Why do we point the one to the example of Christ and assure him that if he will receive the grace of Christ, Christ will enlighten and strengthen and release him, while we present the other with a law, exclude him, and demand obedience to the letter of the law before we admit him? Is it because the one offence shocks us, whilst the other, because it is a besetting sin of our own race, does not shock us? Is it not because our moral sense is perverted and one-sided? The people to whom we go have their own moral scruples; and, if they could exclude us as we exclude them, they would exclude us for showing impatience and racial pride in word and act; they would forbid our dances as we forbid theirs. Is not this sufficient proof that our demands are arbitrary?

Our demands are not only an arbitrary selection, they are not always in themselves unquestionably clear expressions of divine law about which no Christian can have any doubt. Christian missionaries differ, not only as to particular application, but as to the law. From time to time we hear of conferences called to discuss these differences, because of the obvious practical difficulties which arise from disagreement; but uniformity is not attained. Some missionaries lay immense stress upon Sabbath observance as cessation from all work; others regard that as pure Judaism. Some insist upon total abstinence from all forms of alcohol; others decline to do so. Some exclude a man who has more than one wife; some exclude the wives of polygamists; some admit the wives; some admit the man if he puts away all his wives except one; some declare such an action to be immoral and a cause of immorality. The list might be made a long one, for there is hardly to be found one of our demands about which there is universal agreement among all Christian men. But let these suffice to show that we are not agreed, either on the law or on its application. When we are not agreed among ourselves, how can we expect our hearers to accept our demands as divine law, disobedience to which excludes a man from the grace of Christ?

We disagree because we cannot find a definite, clear, explicit command of Christ by which to convince opponents, and sometimes the thing upon which we insist is apparently in direct verbal contradiction to the teaching of Christ; e.g. some of the outcaste tribes of India feed on carrion, and some missionaries forbid that to

Christians. It is easy to understand why they forbid it; but it would be difficult to reconcile their action with the teaching of Christ concerning unclean meats. Sometimes our demands are such that a change of economic conditions would almost seem necessary before they can be properly carried out. We hear missionaries say: 'It is impossible to live a moral life when a whole family, or more than one family, is herded together in a single room.'

If we really believed that the moral demands which we make were of such a character that failure to fulfil them necessarily separated a man from Christ, we should be compelled to treat them as retrospective. But that we do not do. We do not deny the Christianity of Charlemagne because he had more than one wife; we do not deny that our fathers were Christians because they kept slaves; we do not deny that they were Christians because they believed in witchcraft and burnt witches. Then it is possible for a man to do these things without deliberately rejecting Christ, though if one of us did any of them today we should be worthy of excommunication. Thus we admit that our demands are local and temporary, and of our own age and place.

Even in our own age we are not consistent. We exclude men who, before ever they heard the name of Christ, married more than one wife; but we do not openly and publicly excommunicate, and deny Christian burial to, the white fathers of illegitimate half-caste children. Yet the latter case is a far more grievous act of immorality than the former. In the one case there is no impurity of intention, or at any rate impurity of intention is uncertain; in the other it is certain, for no white man thinks that he is serving Christ when he begets these illegitimate children. How we can enforce a law against a man who has acted in ignorance, whilst we condone in act, if not in word, the far worse moral offence of our own fellow-countrymen is simply astounding!

II

The law which we enforce is partial and fragmentary, it is the doubtful, uncertain standard of our own age and race; but we impose it as if it were an explicit divine command, disobedience to which cuts a man off absolutely from the grace of Christ. For how do we enforce it? We make acceptance of our demands the condition of admission into the Christian Church.

We should perhaps hesitate and shrink back and think again about our action if we all realized what that action involves. It means that, *so far as in us lies*, we cut off those whom we reject from the Grace of Christ, and proclaim that Christ has rejected them. We must all acknowledge that the Church ought to receive men whom Christ receives. If then we reject, we can only do so on the ground that we are persuaded that Christ has rejected them. We all acknowledge that there is grace in the communion of the Church: when then we exclude from the Church we deliberately exclude from that grace. We can only do that on the ground that we are persuaded that Christ holds those whom we exclude unfit to receive the grace. We act as if we were sure; but are we quite sure of that?

We exclude hearers and inquirers who come to us seeking Christ, encumbered as they are with the habits and traditions of their people. This is a very different thing from the excommunication of notorious evildoers by the moral conscience of their own people. The Christian character of that act is rooted in the conviction that the sinner is sinning against the light. He is excluded because his offence is a manifest, unmistakable proof that he has wilfully cast himself out, before he is cast out by the Church. His action is so well understood and so universally recognized as evil that he cannot possibly defend it as an act becoming a Christian. That was the ground on which St Paul based his exhortation to the Corinthians to excommunicate the man who had taken his father's wife. Even the Gentiles, he said, know that that is not right.

We reject men who have not offended, and are not offending, against the moral sense of their people. That this is so is proved, not only by the common practice of the country, but by the fact that many Christian natives cannot see for themselves that the act is wicked, and only obey a law which is laid down for them by their foreign teachers. Take, for example, our law of monogamy. We commonly demand that before a man is received into the Church he must put away all his wives except one. Now this is certainly not understood by the great mass of the natives. I have heard a missionary from Central Africa say that when the people hear that a missionary is coming they say: 'Here comes the breaker-up of families.' I asked a native priest in Africa how he justified our law to his own people and he answered: 'I cannot, I simply say that it is the law.' We read that an ' "African Church" movement is growing rapidly in strength and importance in some districts, and threatens to absorb the younger congregations, and to cause division in the older stations. Its power lies in the appeal made to the feeling, widely entertained, that monogamy is a yoke of Western civilization which the African ought not to be called upon to bear.'[1]

From such statements as these it is plain that large numbers of Africans, not only heathen but our own converts, do not understand our insistence upon monogamy in the sense that they perceive clearly that it is impossible to be a Christian and to be a polygamist at the same time.

We are all familiar with the difficulty felt by an African man when he is told that he must discard his wives. What is not so familiar to us, perhaps, is the difficulty of the wife:

> An only wife considers herself placed in an unenviable and humiliating position . . . for the sake of companionship and to secure relief in her daily tasks, the first wife will willingly render assistance in bringing a second wife into the establishment. The average number is from three to five. . . . Where monogamy is the rule, a large number of women must, necessarily, remain unmarried. No Ibo woman would tolerate that position. She would be exposed to every form of contempt and persecution, as well as obliged to suffer the bitter shame of her outraged feelings.[2]

Even we ourselves are often in doubt. I have met missionaries who had grave doubts about the law which they nevertheless felt bound to enforce. Many Christian leaders have told us that we ought to distinguish between low forms of morality and immorality, and that we ought to be careful to avoid confounding the two in the minds of our converts. But our law necessitates the confusion with disastrous results. Take, for instance, the case of Big Hunter. Big Hunter was a chief among the Sioux who fled from the States into Canada and put themselves under the protection of the Canadian Government. Presbyterian missionaries visited them and taught them, and many of them embraced the Christian teaching, and amongst these Big Hunter. He wished to become a Christian, and was told that he must put away all his wives except one. After a long struggle he at last determined to obey, but not knowing how to obey because he did not know how to arrange for his wives, he

[1] CMS *Gleaner*, Dec. 1920, p. 273.
[2] *The East and the West*, Jan. 1920, p. 82.

hanged them. Then he came to the missionaries and told them that he had done what they demanded. Thereupon they drove him away as a murderer, and in despair the man abandoned all hope of ever becoming a Christian, returned to his heathen gods, married two new brides, and lived as a heathen till the day of his death, in spite of the fact that his children became Christians. Those missionaries had maintained the Christian law as they supposed. They had maintained our marriage law: but had they maintained the law of Christ? I have not met a Christian who heard that story without a qualm, or who answered the question whether those missionaries had done right without hesitation.

With less startling consequences we are doing all over the world precisely what these Canadian missionaries did. In some cases the results shock us. Men rejected in Christ's name by us have sometimes done things which appalled us, and women put away in obedience to our law have sometimes fallen into a state which troubled us, and very many who might have been good Christians have come to us seeking Christ, and finding a law have gone back without Christ. It would be a very different matter if the native conscience, unforced by us, excommunicated those who offended against the light. I have already pointed out that a man in England today would be justly excommunicated for acts which our fathers regarded as no sin at all; and as the native Christians grew in knowledge and grace they would certainly learn to consider as grievous crimes things which they, at first, regarded as harmless, or necessary, under the conditions of their life. They would learn to understand the act and to know its real character in relation to the teaching and character of Christ. But that slow growth we have prohibited, preferring to impose our law, and so to attain at once to an apparent immediate advance.

III

In these circumstances it is not surprising that great numbers of natives, both converts and heathen, should look upon the imposition of our rules as the imposition of a yoke of western civilization rather than as a law of Christ. The result is that they are driven into opposition, not only to western civilization, not only to missionaries, but to the truer and higher conception of morality. For instance, in Africa they are driven by our insistence upon monogamy as a formal universal Christian law either into a defence of polygamy or into a rejection of Christianity, or into both. As polygamists they must oppose the teaching of the Christian missionaries. They are driven to fight for polygamy: they must maintain that it is the better way of life for Africans. They must take their place on the wrong side. The choice is a most unhappy one: they must either submit to a yoke and practise a law of which they understand as yet neither the justice nor the expediency, at the command of foreign teachers, or they must adopt an attitude antagonistic to true progress.

That this unhappy choice is set before them is due to the imposition of law. Polygamists might have been on the right side rather than on the wrong. If their wives had not been made the objects of the missionary attack; if, when they learned to believe in Christ, they had been accepted as Christians; the ideal would have been before them not as something inimical, to be hated and dreaded, and resisted, not as a monstrous and tyrannical imposition but as an ideal at which they might safely and wisely look. Many would have shaken their heads at it, but some would have desired it. They would have learned the teaching of Christ with its clear suggestion that monogamy is indeed after the mind of God; they would have heard the teaching of St Paul concerning the relationship of Christ to the Church; they would have compared the homes of monogamists with the homes of polygamists.

As surely as monogamy approved itself to the Christian mind and heart in the West, so surely, and for the same reasons, would it have approved itself to the Christian mind in Africa and the East. Year by year the best men and women, whether polygamists or monogamists themselves, would have been increasingly on its side, many polygamists regretting the contention and trouble in their own homes and warning others against falling into their misfortune, and the monogamists realizing their own higher state and calling others to share it. The battle would perhaps have been long, and its fortune often apparently doubtful, but it need not have been a battle of missionaries against natives, and natives against missionaries, nor need it have been bitter. But this quiet growth we have declined in order to obtain a present immediate victory.

IV

Far more important than even this obvious tactical disadvantage is the conception of the Gospel implied in our insistence upon obedience to an external formal law as a condition precedent to admission into the Church. The first evil is apparent and comparatively superficial; the other is internal and works secretly, and influences our whole work without our perceiving its evil.

If we establish and enforce law as law, whether the principle on which it is based is understood and accepted or not, we make morality to consist in outward obedience to an external law, we present the Church as the guardian of a system of divine laws, we present the Bible as 'a supernatural act of Parliament', we present the way of salvation as the way of obedience to these divine laws.

But none of these things is true. Neither in the Gospels nor in any other part of the New Testament is any code of law laid down. That standard which we so often call the Christian standard of morals, simply does not exist in the New Testament. There is in the New Testament no standard of morals in the sense of a standard external and capable of legal expression, so that we can say that a man who reaches this standard is a Christian, and that a man who fails to reach this standard is not a Christian. The only Christian standard is: 'Thou shalt love the Lord thy God with all thy heart, and with all thy soul and with all thy mind and with all thy strength, and thy neighbour as thyself.' That and none other is the Christian standard of morals. And that is quite incapable of being expressed in a legal code. Anything which can be so expressed by us is a local temporary degraded standard. How degraded the local, temporary standards which we set up really are we cannot know, we can only surmise; but compared with any true Christian ideals they must be infinitely more degraded than is the lowest heathen standard in comparison with ours. The Gospel is certainly not the revelation of a high code of morality.

Christ did not come to men with a new law-book in His hand and assure them that, when they would accept and adopt and carry out the law contained in it, He would accept and bless them. Every attempt to treat any of His sayings as legal enactments has always resulted in confusion, and error, and, what is far worse, in the letting loose of a flood of ill-will, hatred, pride, and self-righteous pharisaism which is the direct contradiction of His Spirit. He came to men not to direct their conduct by external admonitions, but to inspire and to raise them by the presence and power of His Spirit given to them. He did not begin by telling them in detail what the true moral life is

68

and ordering them to follow it. He began by showing it in His own Person and giving to men a Spirit Who should guide and enlighten them until they became like Him.

And so He deals with us now. He comes to us in our degradation and offers us not a law, but His grace. How degraded our state is we do not know. We think of our morals as very high and noble, we compare them with the morals of other men, and we say: 'Ours are Christian morals, theirs are heathen morals; it is impossible for a man to be a Christian unless he accepts our moral code.' If Christ dealt so with us, which of us could be saved? Spiritual pride is a far more deadly sin than concubinage; selfishness is a far more deadly sin than polygamy; hatred is a far more deadly sin than the destruction of twins. Our pride, and selfishness, and hatred, and impurity, express themselves in forms which appear to us less obnoxious than the vices of the heathen; and consequently it is easy for us to denounce their immorality. But if Christ treated us as we treat the heathen, and refused communion with us until we had reformed, what hope should we have?

The revelation of a higher code of morals is no Gospel. By works of law no flesh shall be justified in the sight of God. We are not Christians because we have attained to a standard of morals which can truly be called Christian, but because Christ has given us His Spirit. Our hope now, and for the future, lies not in the attainment of a standard which shall make us fit for His grace; but in the assurance that acceptance of His grace will raise us. We often say that 'His name shall be called Jesus, for He shall save His people from their sins', with the addition: 'not *in* their sin but *from* their sins'. In so saying, whilst we express one truth, we suppress another; for if Christ does not save us *in* our sins we shall never be saved *from* our sins. He comes to us *in* our sins to save us from them. It is of the essence of the Gospel that Christ comes to men in their sins. He came to save sinners.

By our imposition of our moral code, we make obedience to our moral code prior to the reception of Christ and His grace. We insist that men must deliver themselves from conditions which we shrink from, because they are not ours, before we will admit that Christ accepts them, before we will accept them in His name. It is of the essence of the Gospel that Christ came to save those who could not save themselves; it is not the Gospel that He came to save those who could save themselves to a certain extent, and had sufficient courage to risk the enmity of devils whom they feared, and sufficient strength of mind to disregard the public opinion of their people. We preach with our mouths that Christ came to save, but by our action we preach that men must do first for themselves what we say that He came to enable them to do. We tell men that Christ came to give them grace to rise, and we tell them that before they can be raised by Christ's grace they must raise themselves. Christ came to save, not men who had attained to a certain standard of morality, certainly not men who were already prepared to advance to our local, temporary, external standard of morality, but men as He found them. They were to begin by accepting Him and being accepted by Him, and all advance was to be rooted in that.

Obviously we are putting the external before the internal. All that we ask is an external act. We should not dream of telling a man to purify his own soul. The putting away of wives, for instance, does not necessarily involve purification of thought and heart and will; it is sometimes a way of escape from present inconvenience. The motive does not alter the fact. He is now a monogamist, therefore we can receive him; or, he is still a polygamist, therefore we must reject him. We cannot deal with the inward things; we can only act on the outward facts. But the one thing that really matters is the attitude of the man's soul to Christ, and the indwelling of the Holy Spirit. When then we make the bare external obedience to a formal external law the first thing, we teach all men to regard the external as the chief matter; and unfortunately that is exactly what human beings are only too ready to do. To deal with the outward things is to lose the way, and to lead others out of the way; Christ deals with the inward things. From inward purification springs all progress.

v

This question is not now raised for the first time. In the days of St Paul there was a strong party in the Church which insisted that before converts from heathen religions could be admitted into the Church they must be compelled to accept and to practise the moral code of the Christians in Jerusalem. The morals of Phrygians and Pamphylians, of Greeks and Romans, were in their eyes utterly degraded. Marriage was in many parts of the empire no more than a temporary alliance; concubinage was almost universal; fornication was not even considered a vice; prostitution was not only condoned by religious men but had a place in their religious rites; and vices even more disgusting were commonly practised.

To preach salvation in Christ to such people without binding them to the moral law might have seemed both absurd and iniquitous. Men might have argued (1) That it was worse than that, it was flat disobedience to Christ Himself who taught: 'The scribes and Pharisees sit in Moses's seat; all therefore whatsoever they bid you observe, that observe and do,'[1] and: 'One jot or one tittle shall in no wise pass from the Law till all be fulfilled.'[2] It was disobedience to His precept; it was also the repudiation of His example. He Himself observed the Law. No one, not even His enemies, had attempted to prove that He broke the Law or undermined its authority. Even St Paul in his controversy with the judaizing party never argued that Christ had overthrown the Law or had told His disciples that they need not keep it. How then could the Gospel be preached without the Law? Could men accept Christ and follow Him, and not accept and follow the Law which He accepted and obeyed? How could men be united to a Christ who was Himself within the Covenant of God's people whilst they themselves were not within the Covenant?

(2) To teach men to believe in Christ without enforcing obedience to the Law would be to ensure the divorce of Christian faith from Christian morals. If it were possible to preach Christ without preaching also the moral Law, then these two could be separated in thought and in practice. They could be distinguished one from the other. To be a Christian it would be no longer necessary to keep the Law. Is Christ the minister of sin? Christ and holiness of life are inseparable. To talk of preaching Christ without enforcing obedience to the Law is to separate the inseparable.

(3) It would be futile to tell the converts to lead moral lives without giving them the hedge of the Law. The Jews themselves needed the Law to direct them even at home; and abroad they needed it still more. Heathen converts living in an atmosphere of heathenism could not possibly be expected to maintain any moral standard unless they had that support which even Jews, with centuries of moral teaching behind them, needed. If new converts bore in their bodies the mark of their dedication to the moral life, if they associated as closely as

---

[1] St Matt. 23. 2, 3.
[2] St Matt. 5. 18.

possible with those who through long centuries of discipline had learnt the importance of a high moral standard, they might learn to stand; but without that support they must fall. The temptations of their surroundings, the inherited tendencies of their race, would be too strong. Christian morals would be no better than heathen morals.

(4) That must react upon the Church at home. Even if Jewish Christians avoided as far as possible contact with these immoral heathen Christians, the mere fact that men who were not bound by the Law had been admitted into the Church would involve acceptance of the principle that men could be saved in Christ without the Law. If some could be saved in Christ without the Law, then none need keep the Law. If a heathen could be saved in Christ without accepting the Law, a Jew could be saved in Christ if he abandoned the Law. The observance of the Law was certainly a burden; some would certainly shake it off. Then there would be Jewish Christians living like heathen, and the Church would have abandoned the principle on which alone they could be rebuked and restored. To admit uncircumcised men into the Church was not so much to extend the Gospel to the heathen as to forsake the way of holiness.

Not only the religious privileges of the Jews, but the example of Christ, the teaching of Christ, the foundations of all morality were to be abandoned in order that the way might be made easy for men of licentious life to become Christians in name, and escape from a yoke which every Jew, and every proselyte, knew that they ought to bear.

These are not light considerations; they might well make men pause, and every one of these arguments might have been used by the Jewish party in Jerusalem with as great a force and propriety as they can be urged by us in favour of insisting upon obedience to our moral Law today. Yet no argument which the judaizing party could present availed. To maintain the supremacy of faith in Christ, St Paul refused to enforce the Law; and despite all the efforts of judaizing missionaries the Church was established in Christ. Christ is the only Saviour; the moral law is no saviour. Men are not saved by Christ and the moral law; they are saved in Christ. They are to be admitted into Christ's Church, not because they have accepted a new moral code, but because they believe in Christ. Christ is supreme.

St Paul maintained the supremacy of Christ, and the history of the churches of the West proved how little truth there was in all those apparently weighty considerations. For a time indeed men might well quake at the moral condition of the church as it appeared outwardly in a city like Corinth, but Christ triumphed. Faith in Christ produced a higher morality than the legal code, the abandonment of which seemed to shake the very foundations of all morality.

VI

It almost seems to be a rule of Christian progress that to ascend men must first apparently descend. To know the power of Christ, individual men must make that fearful descent which consists in forsaking the attempt to make themselves righteous, they must abandon the hope that they can attain to righteousness by their obedience to law whether written in their conscience or taught to them by authority. That is an appalling adventure. It seems like a contradiction, a very reversal, of our nature, a denial of ourselves. Yet how many generations of Christian men have proved it!

So to know the power of Christ it seems that the Church must make a like adventure in its missionary work, and cast away its righteousness in order that it may appear again as the grace of Christ alone. How terrible that adventure seems is shown by our reluctance to face it. '*We must*,' we say, 'maintain the Christian standard of morality.' We cannot. It does not lie with us. Morality for us as Christians should be truth in the inward parts. And that we cannot maintain. All that we can do is to enforce an external law; and that we must not do. But because we say we *must*, we do exactly that very thing which we condemn the judaizing Christians for doing; and we come near to committing that very fault which we applaud St Paul for opposing.

In Islam there is a fixed standard of morals, there is a definite external code; yet Muslims can and do accept men before they have learnt that code or advanced to that standard, in the belief that they will learn. They do learn to grow up to the standard, but when once they have attained, they have attained. Herein lies the secret of the stagnation of Islam: it has a moral standard. It can raise men up to that standard, and after that—nothing. There is no infinite advance. If we set up and maintain a standard of Christian morals embodied in a code so far as in us lies, we invite a like disaster. In Christ there is no such standard, but the promise of infinite progress. Inspired by Christ's Spirit, strengthened by His grace, converts

73

from heathenism will advance not to our present Western standard, but far beyond it. The imposition of our present standard may seem to us for the moment to give us and our converts some advantage, but it saps the spring of future progress.

That is what I fear. We have begun by imposing a system of external rules, and we cannot easily go back. In the beginning it would have been comparatively easy to have avoided the difficulty. To have baptized men who confessed Christ without insisting that they must first accept our laws, to have established churches in native villages under their own elders without breaking up their social order, would no more have been a lowering of our standard of morality than the establishment of a kindergarten class in a school is a lowering of the standard of education in the school. But now it would appear to many a definitely retrograde step. Yet it should be made. It is one of those fearful acts of faith in Christ which Christ at times demands of His followers; it is one of those acts of abandonment of our own righteousness which make way for the revelation of His power.

VII

One thing at least is certain: as long as we continue to teach and enforce our law as law, as long as we make acceptance of it a condition precedent to admission into the Church, so long we can expect no spontaneous growth. For it is unquestionable that unless those who receive a new moral law from an external source can fully understand both its moral necessity and how to apply it under the conditions in which they live, insistence upon its acceptance and practice by an external authority must inevitably check spontaneous advance.

Suppose that missionaries came to us from a higher sphere, and regarding our moral condition as we regard the moral condition of 'raw heathen', began by insisting that, before we could be admitted into communion with them, we must abandon once and for all our heathen practices. Suppose, for instance, that they began by insisting that we should conduct all our businesses with a single eye to the salvation of all whom we employed and all with whom we dealt, or that in the education of our children we should think solely of the service of Christ and not at all of their social, or economic, advantage; suppose that they treated an impatient or hasty temper as sufficient cause for excommunication; suppose that they laid down rules for our direction in these matters and demanded the cancelling of any contracts or engagements into which we had previously entered, and declined to recognize us as Christians until we had done so. Such missionaries would be acting precisely as we act when we insist that a man must reform his social relations in accordance with our ideas of moral life before he can be admitted to baptism. But should we not be amazed and confounded, and question whether it was possible for most of us whilst we lived on this earth to become Christians; and if we desire to propagate such teaching should we not be confronted with almost insuperable difficulties?

So long as we hold to this doctrine it is impossible for us to establish churches on the apostolic model. If Africans, Chinese and Indians can have no churches of their own until they have satisfied us that they are so established in our system of morals that they will enforce it themselves; obviously we must govern them and guide them for a very long time; obviously we cannot possibly commit to them authority to establish churches. We must keep that authority secure in our own hands, for the churches which they established might not see that our morals were Christian. All progress must be carefully kept within the limits imposed by our capacity to supply governors.

There is only one alternative, and that is to set before men the example of Christ, and the law of Christ which is the only standard of Christian morality: 'Thou shalt love the Lord thy God with all thy heart and with all thy soul and with all thy strength and with all thy mind, and thy neighbour as thyself.' If Big Hunter[1] had been taught that law, he would have accepted it gladly and would have tried to keep it by loving his wives, and as the people advanced in knowledge they would speedily have accepted the teaching that the best way to fulfil Christ's law in respect of wives is to have only one. When we teach a law which is less than Christ's law, when we set up a standard of morality which is lower than Christ's standard, we often fail to attain even that standard which we set up; and because we have put the letter in the place of the spirit we ourselves miss the spirit in enforcing the letter. We have laid down the law and passed over the love of God; we have set our hearers on the wrong path; we have raised up a most serious barrier to the spontaneous expansion of the Church.

[1] p. 65.

CHAPTER 6

Civilization and Enlightenment

When we went abroad as missionaries we went to peoples who were ignorant of Christ; and, naturally, their civilization or barbarism was not Christian in origin or in character. Their social customs were rooted in heathen ideas, and were sometimes extremely cruel and brutish. Obviously, we were compelled to decide at once our attitude to this heathen social order, in relation to ourselves, our converts, and the heathen to whom we went as missionaries.

For ourselves we decided that it was impossible for us to dwell among the people, sharing their life. Even if it had been physically possible, it would have seemed like descending from heaven to share the sinful life of wicked men; we should have felt that we were partakers of their sins. Neither would we be nomads, wandering teachers, passing from town to town, and village to village, pausing here a while, and there a while, to instruct any who would listen. We settled permanently, we acquired land, we built houses, we established mission stations over against the people. To these stations we brought out our wives; in them we made our homes. Outwardly and inwardly these mission compounds were little bits of England transplanted into a foreign country. Within their walls was a European civilization; outside was a heathen civilization or barbarism. When a man crossed the threshold of a mission compound, he stepped from one world into another, from one age into another. Many a weary traveller has described them for us, and expressed the delight which he felt in passing for a moment into these homes of quiet, order, cleanliness and decency, before he plunged again into the barbarism outside.

When the early missionaries built the first houses in those compounds, they were taking a step which must have seemed of the simplest and most commonplace character. They must have houses; they must have houses fit for Europeans to live in. What could be more obvious! Yet, in building those houses they fixed the character and the limits of mission work in that country for a century, perhaps for two or three centuries. Those houses represented a spirit, they revealed the relationship which was to be between the missionary and the people. They argued the immobility of the Christian force; they prophesied that European missionaries would still be there a hundred years later, calling themselves missionaries still, ministering to the third and fourth generations of Christians. They proclaimed that the missionaries would not be men wholly given to the preaching of a religion alone, but that they would consider the introduction of their civilization a large part of their work, and new converts would accept a new civilization as part of their new religion. They foretold a history: the spread of the religion would be as easy and as difficult as the multiplication of houses like those. Europeans would propagate it in proportion as they could multiply such places, natives would as easily propagate it as they could multiply houses like those. The policy of the missionary society, the history of the Church, would be controlled more by the existence of that house than by anything that happened in the native village. The house was there before the converts.

I

From these compounds we went out into the country round to preach and teach, and we cultivated the closest possible relations with the people compatible with this distinction; and going outside we met at once the heathen customs, and all the misery and vice which heathen customs engender. We preached, and we taught, and we made converts. When a man became an inquirer, what were we to tell him? The customs were in our eyes obviously contrary to the Gospel, as we understood it. Were we to be content to leave him to find that out for himself, or were we to insist upon his abandoning them at once? We had no doubt whatever which was the right course to pursue: we forbade the customs: we could not tolerate them for a moment: we could not suffer anyone who called himself a Christian to tolerate them for a moment.

Instantly the position of the converts became exceedingly difficult. Often they were persecuted, or even driven from their homes, or villages. What then were we to do? Was it possible for us to sit by and see our converts persecuted and make no effort to save them? They were being persecuted certainly as Christians but also because they obeyed our directions. In some cases by merely opening the doors of the compound to them they would be saved from death. In

77

some cases the exercise of a little personal influence with the native authorities would save them; in some cases an appeal to a European Governor would bring the protection of civil and military force. Inevitably we became the protectors, the patrons, the employers of our converts; equally inevitably they learned to depend upon us.

Cut off from the social life of their own people by prohibitions, which their fellows could not understand at all, and which they themselves did not understand very well, cast adrift from all their familiar organization and authority, they were lost. Men cannot live without some social order. Obviously we could not simply destroy, we must construct some new order, we must teach them some customs to take the place of those which they had cast off. There was no time for them to create a Christian social order of their own. They could not gradually transform heathen customs into Christian customs as we had done in our own history; for our conscience had forbidden that. We must teach and they must learn a new social order at once. What customs could we teach them? Plainly only Christian customs, that is, the customs of the Christian compound. In other words they must adopt our civilization as far as they possibly could. Only poverty and ignorance prevented them from becoming exact imitations of us. Whatever we told them was a good custom. Whatever custom they saw us practise, they followed without question, indiscriminately, unless it caused them too much inconvenience; but they did not understand what they were doing. The new civilization had no root.

The missionaries who went abroad a century ago were not so learned in hygiene as we of this day, and one of the evil customs which troubled them was savagery in dress and the indecency of nakedness. They were well instructed in the shame of Adam and Eve. A Christian naked, or savagely clad, seemed to them a horrible compound of light and darkness. They clothed their converts, and taught them to know their shame. European clothes became then, and still remain, the symbol of our denationalizing influence.

Today many of our missionaries loudly proclaim that they do not wish to see their converts denationalized, that they do not want to see them abandoning all their native customs. They boast that their converts wear native clothes and live a native life, and they strive to restore native games, dances and music. They strive to restore again much that earlier missionaries destroyed.

But the real problem is not whether we should encourage or discourage any particular custom, but whether we should be the judges of what is fitting; not whether we should retain or revive this or that native custom, but whether we should touch these things directly at all. To revoke the prohibitions and impositions of our predecessors and to set up or to maintain others, is really in principle to do precisely what they did.[1] They accepted the position of judges of native customs; they were sure that it was their duty to decide whether a custom could be tolerated, whether they were, or were not, to forbid their converts to practise it, and they fulfilled that duty to the best of their ability and knowledge. They entered upon a most difficult and dangerous path; and, if they made mistakes we shall certainly make as many if we try to do the same thing.

The only alternative is to abandon altogether that position, and to admit that we cannot judge. We must begin with positive teaching, not with negative prohibitions, and be content to wait and to watch whilst the native Christians slowly recreate their own customs, as the Spirit of Christ gradually teaches them to transform what today is heathen, and tomorrow, purged of its vice, will appear as a Christian custom, just as the Saturnalia was transformed into the Christian feast of the Incarnation. But that involves the retracing of the path which to our fathers seemed essentially the right one. It means that Christian converts must be left at first in their heathen surroundings and must live as their people, and be still of their people, until they grow so strong in numbers and in knowledge that they will be able to correct what is false, and to amend what is evil, with that full understanding which is born of slow and quiet interior advance. It means that we cannot force them at a bound to adopt or reject at our command, even when the adoption or rejection seems to be an immense immediate step forward. If we are not prepared to do that, if we still accept the position of judges, and prohibit customs or restore them, to differ from the judgements of our predecessors and to build again the things which we destroyed is simply to reveal our incapacity to judge truly, and to make ourselves transgressors.

[1] At a Conference held at Le Zoute in September 1926, Dr Richter said: 'I am more and more conscious that those decisions were taken by our predecessors in greater or less ignorance. They did not know what those customs meant, they did not know the Africans. We know the facts far better than they knew them, and cannot but ask ourselves, shall we continue to follow their rules?'—*The Christian Mission in Africa*, p. 49.

In relation to the heathen we attacked the customs directly. For this end we had one powerful weapon, education. We established schools. By means of the education given in our schools we hoped to teach the budding and more pliant youth Christian doctrine and Christian customs; we hoped to make converts; we hoped to educate and raise up a strong and enlightened Christian Church; we hoped to teach the evil consequences of heathen customs, and so to reform society.

We succeeded. We did uproot some of the more terrible and evil heathen customs. But the Christians educated in our schools were still more widely separated from their countrymen, and the heathen educated by us in our high schools and colleges were not converted in any large numbers, and were sometimes shrewd critics of the Western civilization, of which they had adopted the outward symbols, and of the doctrine which they had refused to accept.

II

Nor was the adoption of these methods of propagating our religion without its effect upon us. The establishment of schools and hospitals, especially, perhaps, of the larger schools and hospitals and colleges in great centres, altered our conception of our work as missionaries. They called out large numbers of mission workers of a new type with new ideas of missionary work. We began to hear such phrases as these: the gospel of enlightenment, the gospel of healing, the social gospel, and, in later years, the gospel of sex equality. Whilst we continued to speak of our medical and educational work in the old way as designed to open doors and attract hearers, and to convert, we began also to speak of medical, educational and social work as forms of preaching the Gospel. The uplift of the people was a gospel in itself. Christ came to raise mankind, and to raise mankind out of the slough of superstition and evil conditions was, we argued, to preach and to practise His Gospel. In the event, by raising the whole race, such missionary work was preparing for the day when races and tribes and peoples instructed in Christian ethics, strengthened by Christian science, enriched by Christian sociology, would recognize the source of all this blessing, and would be able to worship and serve Christ duly as Christians ought to do.

We practised the same theory in England in an age of great social upheaval. Social service was a cry which held and attracted large numbers of the younger and the abler Christian minds, and to a very great extent the Church threw herself into this work. A church was scarcely considered complete without large institutions, guilds, clubs, halls. And all these things were urged upon the generosity of churchmen on the assurance that their provision would prepare the way for Christ.

We have now had many years' experience of that method of approach, and it is becoming increasingly plain, it is, indeed, already commonly acknowledged, that the Church has not, by these social activities, brought men in any great degree within the sphere of its spiritual influence. It has not succeeded along this road in imparting that spiritual life which it exists to minister. Many deplore the obvious fact that, while the institutions have done much valuable work, the great mass of those who have used them have not drawn nearer to the Church or to Christ. The churches which supported them most strongly have increased neither in number nor in spiritual power in anything like the proportion which the energy thrown into this social work presupposed.

This is not really surprising; for it is extremely easy to divorce social reform and the alleviation of suffering from religion. How easily they can be divorced is proved by the common fact that both at home and abroad the Church is being supplanted in these social activities by governments which promote education, and support hospitals and schemes of industrial reform subsidized from public funds without any religious purpose. Social reform is not necessarily Christian, and schemes for the amelioration of the conditions of life certainly do not necessarily lead men to Christ, even if they are set on foot by Christian men with the most serious Christian intention.

III

Both at home and in the mission field the change in our thought was more important than any change in our method of work. In the mission field the more we emphasized the gospel of enlightenment and social reform, the more these things tended to take the first place in our thoughts. In the beginning we put Christ first. Belief in Christ was the one thing needful. Out of that belief health and enlightenment and reform would inevitably grow. If we were not quite sure of that, we were, at least, sure that these things were secondary, and must follow. Conversion to Christ was the first thing, the only thing that really mattered, and our attention must be given first and before all else to leading men to Christ. But more and more as we developed these social activities they became first in time, and two serious consequences followed.

(1) Putting intellectual, moral and social advance first in time, we inevitably tended to accept the position that reform of conditions was a necessary antecedent to the living of a Christian life. We had, as I have already pointed out, certain convictions as to the meaning of the term 'Christian Life'. A 'Christian life' was a life separated from all heathen practices, it was a life of civilized Christian decency as we understood it. It was a life as nearly after our pattern as possible. We were then, and we are now, utterly incapable of conceiving, or recognizing, Christian life under barbarous conditions. Consequently, we naturally spoke often as if it were impossible to live a Christian life in bad surroundings. We heard men say that some reform was of pressing importance, because it was impossible for men to live a Christian life under such conditions. Or from another point of view, as a missionary from India expressed it to me the other day, it is impossible for those people in their ignorance and degradation to receive our message until they are freed from the bondage and degradation in which they are kept by their overlords.

That is a very serious position to adopt. It subordinates Christ to conditions. Historically, it is not true. Men in those conditions have become Christians, and very good Christians too, before the conditions of their life were changed, not only in India, but elsewhere. I suppose it is difficult to imagine any conditions more repugnant to all that we call Christian life than the conditions in which many slaves lived in heathen households in the Roman Empire, subject absolutely to the will of their masters; yet they became Christians and lived Christian lives in those conditions.

In the mission field we need to revise our ideas of the meaning of Christian life. A Christian life is a life lived in Christ: it does not depend upon conditions. I mean that the life of a slave-girl, the concubine of a savage heathen, amidst the most cruel and barbarous surroundings, herself the instrument of the most vicious and immoral practices, may be a truly Christian life. Christ transcends all conditions.

And Christ transcends all ignorance. It will be observed that my friend from India said that ignorance was a bar preventing the people from receiving our message. That may very well be. Our message is not delivered in a form easy to be understood by men of no literary education, nor is it always delivered by men who can approach their hearers with true understanding and use the expressions which they naturally understand. But that the most ignorant man on earth cannot receive Christ and find grace and help in Him seems to me to be contradicted by our own knowledge of Christ's nature and our frequent experience of His power.

(2) If intellectual moral and social advance is put first in time, before the acceptance of faith in Christ, it is obvious that this intellectual enlightenment and moral and social advance must be based upon some other foundation than faith in Christ; and if it is expected that this enlightenment and improvement will issue in the acceptance of faith in Christ, it is obvious that faith in Christ is not the foundation but the coping stone of social and moral progress. When we accept the idea that we must work first for the intellectual, moral and social advancement of those to whom we go as missionaries, we inevitably tend to accept that conclusion.

And yet we all know well that intellectual enlightenment may be put to serve the worst ends, and become the instrument of its own destruction, unless it is directed by Christ. We all know that social improvement, sought for its own sake, may be a like cause of disaster. We all know that moral progress, sought for itself, may be a source of spiritual pride, and a cause of spiritual blindness which may end in its own perdition. We all know that for ourselves we look for no progress but in the gift of Christ's grace, and that all seeming progress which is not rooted in Christ is for us a snare and a delusion. When we think, as Christians ought to think, in terms of the eternal, we know the truth; and even in terms of the seen and the temporal, we have every good reason for knowing that what the world calls progress is built on very unstable foundations. Wars proclaim it.

To follow this path must lead to failure. 'Seek ye first,' said Christ, 'the kingdom of God and His righteousness, and all these things shall be added unto you.' Putting intellectual enlightenment and social reform first in time, we have, by deeds which speak louder than words, taught men to seek 'all these things' first, and some today justify their action by identifying intellectual enlightenment and social and political reform with the Kingdom of God and His Righteousness. To identify the Kingdom of God and His Righteousness with social and political doctrines always has led, and always must lead, to disaster. The Kingdom of God and His Righteousness are founded in Christ, but these doctrines and reforms can easily be divorced from Christ, and are pursued by many who own no allegiance to Christ.

When we seek social advancement and intellectual enlightenment first we set men on the wrong path. We set them on a path which ends with human powers. If we look at the history of the world we see civilizations rise and rise until the human powers seem to be worn out with their own efforts after material and intellectual advancement, and then they fall. This is expressed in the Chinese saying: 'Rise to the top and you must descend.' Only in Christ is the promise of infinite progress.

This 'Christian' civilization, this 'Christian enlightenment' which can be divorced from faith in Christ, and assimilated by non-Christians, is severely limited. We talk of 'Christian social conditions', 'Christian civilization', as something which we know and can impart to others; but in truth we do not know what Christian civilization is. It is an ideal towards which Christians strive: it is something infinitely remote from us, and we do not know what it is in its beauty; only we know that it is in Christ and is to be attained in Him by learning of Him. That knowledge cannot be imparted to non-Christians; the only Christian civilization which we can impart directly to others is the civilization of Christian England, Western Civilization. But that is not Christian Civilization. To teach men this is indeed to mislead them. Very often the heathen see its iniquity more clearly than we do. If men learn to confound the teaching of Christ with western civilization they may well shrink from both. But when we use the terms 'Christian civilization' and 'our civilization', or 'our customs', or 'our social doctrines' as convertible terms, and teach our customs and our social doctrines as 'Christian' to those to whom we go as missionaries, we are always on the verge of this danger, and when we attempt to uplift a whole people, Christian and non-Christian alike, by introducing them, we are in fact falling into it.

If we set Christ first, faith in Christ first, the Name of Christ first, we set men on a sure road to something that is infinitely good, but that progress is in Christ, not in our intellectual, moral, and social doctrines, and we cannot set them on that path except by bringing them to Christ. We must put Christ first.

I know that missionaries will say—Oh, but we do put Christ first. I answer that this theory which leads us to put intellectual enlightenment and social reform first in time is a direct contradiction of it. The point where we Christians differ from other men is that we know the prime cause of all true progress and can therefore show the true path: others see only secondary causes, and, therefore, can only deal with secondary causes. The prime cause of all human misery and ignorance is spiritual, the prime cause of all progress is spiritual renewal by the Spirit of Christ. When, then, we follow those who see only secondary causes, social conditions and the like, and treat these secondary causes first, as if they were the real prime causes of progress, we forsake our true function. The fact that in our heart of hearts we know the first cause, that in out heart of hearts we are assured that faith in Christ is the beginning and foundation of all true progress, does not alter the fact that when we deal first with the secondary things we present to others secondary causes of progress as sufficient; and no words that we can use will correct the evidence of our acts. We have in fact gone astray, however stoutly we may deny it. In our presentation of civilization, as in our presentation of doctrine and of morals, there is one common defect: in each case we present something less than Christ.

IV

If we read St Paul's argument in the first two chapters of the First Epistle to the Corinthians we find a singular and illuminating expression of his attitude towards human aids to the preaching of the Gospel. He is speaking of a philosophical presentation of the Gospel to a people who delighted in philosophy; and he says that he deliberately avoided it. The reasons which he gives are these:

(1) The use of it might make void the Cross (1 Cor. 1. 17). It would conceal the truth that what was a stumbling-block and foolishness to Jews and Greeks revealed in itself the power and the wisdom of God. The fact that it appeared foolishness to men made the wisdom of God manifest. If it had appeared wisdom to men it would have remained a wisdom of men in their eyes. Only by appearing foolishness could it reveal a wisdom of God which confounded the wisdom of men.

(2) As foolishness in the eyes of men it could be accepted only by those who were prepared to accept what appeared to the wise of the

85

world foolishness. Consequently it was commonly rejected by the wise and mighty, and accepted by the foolish and the weak (1. 26, 27). This, which to a hasty glance seemed to be a dishonour and a failure, revealed still more clearly the wisdom and power of God; for if the Gospel triumphed in spite of its apparent foolishness, and in spite of the obvious weakness and ignorance of its believers, in accomplishing that which no wisdom of men in the hands of the wisest and mightiest could accomplish, then the power and wisdom was seen to be of God alone, and there was no place for man's glory, or for the glorification of his wisdom and prudence. The Glory was Christ's alone (1. 28–31).

(3) The faith of the converts was established on a true foundation (2. 5). If they had been attracted and convinced by an argument which appealed to the human intellect they might have been able to found their faith on a philosophy of the same character and maintained on grounds similar to those on which other religious philosophies were based. They would have believed, because the Christian philosophy seemed secure and its exposition irrefutable. That is the basis on which men naturally accept any doctrine taught to them. The doctrine stands or falls with the intellectual argument which expresses it. Any doctrine, any religious conviction, based on that foundation, must always stand in the power of the human intellect. What human intelligence can set up human intelligence may overturn. At any moment a human argument may be met by a stronger argument, and when so met it must give way, even though the stronger argument is only a negative argument. St Paul was determined (2. 2) that Christian faith, so far as he was concerned, should rest on no such fragile basis. He would have Christian faith rest on nothing else than the power of God, which bows and dominates the whole personality, not intellect alone, but will and emotion also, and seizes and holds the man who is subject to it with a power which no human argument can touch. The love of the Cross, the terror of the Cross, is not to be confined by an intellectual argument. Belief which results from the apprehension of that revelation of the Divine Nature is not to be established on any such basis as a human philosophy; and therefore St Paul rejected any statement of the Divine Reality which might lead men to accept a doctrine instead of surrendering themselves to the control of a divine power. He manifested the Spirit, he demonstrated the power, and he led men as they

experienced these to welcome and accept the Cross in which they were revealed.

(4) A Christian philosophy followed (2. 7–16), a philosophy deeper than any philosophy known to men, as based not on an intellectual foundation, nor speaking only to the intellect, but embracing the whole personality of man and leading the whole man to apprehend and embrace that love of Christ and that truth of Christ which is supremely revealed in the Cross; a philosophy which spoke in terms of spirit, moved by a Spirit, the Spirit of Christ, the Holy Spirit; a philosophy in which Divine Love expressed itself; a philosophy which appeared to the wise men of the world as foolish as the teaching on which it was founded, because it could never be adequately expressed, still less explained, in human language, to a human intellect which had not itself shared in the administration of the Spirit which inspired it. St Paul knew the love of the Cross, the terror of the Cross. He induced rather than argued the conviction which followed his teaching; and then among those who knew the power of the Cross, and among them only, could the wisdom of God in the Cross be spoken or understood. The philosophy followed the revelation of God in Christ to the faith of the believers, a philosophy absurd to any but to believers in Christ. It is impossible to make any man who does not know the power of the Cross understand the wisdom of God revealed in the Cross; but by those who do know that power the wisdom can be set forth to others who know it.

This, as I understand it, is something of the meaning of this passage of St Paul's epistle to the Corinthians; but before I go further I want to repeat that what is most certain is that the Apostle deliberately rejected any means of propagating the faith which might distract men in any way from the truth that Christian faith is founded not in a human philosophy but in the power of God. Any human assistance which might lead men to found their faith on any human skill or wit he put aside, and he put it aside deliberately, not because he had it not in his power to use it, but because he would not.

Now I suggest that the place which philosophy held in popular estimation in St Paul's day is held in ours by Science, not Science in its technical sense only, but in its wider sense, as when we talk of the Science of Education, or of Medicine, or of Sociology, or of Hygiene. It is this Science in the wide sense which we put first when we talk of social reform and the permeation of society with Christian ideals as the way to the establishment of the faith.

First then I would ask, if we look at this Science on which we so largely rely, and attempt to place it in St Paul's statement, where does it naturally take its place? Does it not belong essentially to that which he calls the wisdom of the wise, the wisdom of the world? Is it not in fact the wisdom of the world of our day; is it not the wisdom of the wise of our day? I think it is hardly possible for anyone to deny that it is.

Then does not his argument apply? Is there no danger that the presentation of the Gospel of Christ by means of a Science which is unquestionably the wisdom of the wise may produce exactly that effect which the Apostle sought to avoid?

(1) Does it not conceal the foolishness of the Cross? The triumph of the Cross is the triumph of the Cross because it is not the triumph of anything else, and it cannot be the triumph of the Cross if it is the triumph of anything else. If our preaching and teaching of Western science is, as it manifestly is, a triumph for Western science, if we constantly hear our missionaries talk of the spread of Christian civilization and Christian enlightenment among peoples who are not Christian; is there not a danger that the Science, the wisdom of men, is taking the place of the wisdom of God? Does not the teaching of the wisdom of men deprive the Gospel of the Cross of that foolishness which is its glory? The salvation of men, body, soul and spirit is not seen as the revelation of God's wisdom through the foolishness of preaching, but as the revelation of the wisdom of men who devised such wonderful and uplifting schemes. If a non-Christian looks at the progress of Christians in heathen lands today, does he not often ascribe their progress to the wisdom of men? Do not our own missionaries often say that without this wisdom of men, this scientific education, this social doctrine, there is no hope for the advancement of converts? I do not want to labour the point. This argument of St Paul certainly does apply.

(2) In our use of the wisdom of this world we naturally appeal to the wise men and the mighty and expect them to receive this wisdom. It is one of the great arguments most commonly used on behalf of our great scientific institutions abroad that by them alone we can reach those educated and governing classes, who will not listen to the preaching of the Cross. We use the appeal of Science

most vigorously in our preaching to the educated, for they are likely to understand and receive that appeal. For the most part they do accept this wisdom of men. The wisdom of men appeals to them and satisfies them, so far as any wisdom of men can satisfy a human soul. Men who remain non-Christians accept this wisdom, and sometimes practise it, and then we point to them as notable examples of the success of our work. From such and such a mission school went out this wise Governor, that great doctor, the other highly paid official, whose success all men admire. But is there here a revelation of the wisdom of God, or of the wisdom of men? Is there here glory given to God or glory given to men? The triumph of Christian ideals and ideas in the person of these men is the triumph of ideals and ideas which can be held by non-Christian men. Where then is the glory of the Cross, the glory of Christ, the glory of God? If the wisdom of God is revealed when the weak confound the mighty, here the mighty enter upon their own inheritance. Surely it is true to say that St Paul's argument applies here also.

(3) Do we not attempt to establish faith in Christ upon it? Do we not indeed proclaim that we undertake all our social, industrial, intellectual, teaching and practice as a means to lead men to faith in Christ? It would be a totally different matter if Christians, to express their love for men, inaugurated Land Banks, introduced better seed and better agricultural methods than those previously known, established schools for the blind or deaf, or hospitals for the sick, and taught arts and sciences in colleges. Such action might be compared to the action of the Good Samaritan, who, finding a neighbour in need, helped him. But we do not do our work simply like that: we proclaim that the introduction and establishment of these arts and sciences are the steps preliminary to the acceptance of the gospel, and that we carry on our institutional work for that purpose. Society must be permeated with Christian ideas, and then men will accept Christ; the ignorant must be taught scientifically in our modern educational way and then they will be able to accept Christ; social abuses must be reformed and then men will be able to accept Christ; social ethics must be inculcated and then men will be able to accept Christ. To teach agricultural improvements to poor agriculturalists that they may become better agriculturalists, or engineering to men that they may become good engineers, is one thing: to teach men these things that they may become Christians is another. It

is precisely what St Paul, as I understand him, refused to do.

Just as in St Paul's day a doctrine was expected to stand or fall with the strength or the weakness of the intellectual argument with which it was supported; so today a doctrine popularly stands or falls with the present material advantages which follow its practice. When, then, we link together in the closest association our civilization and our religious belief, when we talk of our Christian civilization, our Christian sociology, our Christian education, our Christian enlightenment, are we not teaching men to try our Gospel by our social conditions, our enlightenment, our civilization, and to accept or to reject it on that basis? A speaker at the Washington Foreign Missions Convention in 1925 warned us: 'To allow the impression to become fixed that Western civilization and Christianity are not only identical terms, but that the one is the fruit of the other, is for ever to block the way for an understanding of Christ and the Gospel.' That is not perhaps very clearly expressed, but is he not warning us that men are confounding our civilization with Christianity, and that to give occasion for such an error is disastrous? Sooner or later men begin to see the faults in our civilization; and if they have confounded the teaching of Christ with our civilization they may well shrink from both; and the faith of those who have accepted our teaching may well be shaken when they see that the Christian civilization which we have set before them is liable to serious attack.

That is what we see today in Africa, in India, in China. I sometimes wonder, when I hear men speak of the contribution which our foreign missions bring to us at home, whether they reckon among the gifts of that contribution the searching criticism to which those to whom we go preaching the Gospel subject our Christian civilization. It is to my mind one of the most valuable. But if we have, as I fear that we have, really taught multitudes to confound our civilization with Christianity, then surely we have fallen into that error which St Paul was determined to avoid. The Christian civilization which we hoped would prepare the way for Christ has proved itself a stumbling-block, and we must confess that we have gone astray, and have obscured the true foundation, the Cross of Christ which is itself the condemnation of our civilization. Our Western enlightenment, our Christian social doctrines, our Christian science, are no foundation upon which to build faith in Christ.

But some missionary may say, What are you talking about? We

do not build the faith of our converts on our social and intellectual enlightenment: *post hoc* is not necessarily *propter hoc*. That is true. If St Paul had preached philosophy it does not necessarily follow that the faith of his converts would have been founded on the philosophy. In many cases it would not have been so founded. He was afraid that it might in some cases be so, and he was determined that there should be no cause of it in him. I suggest that we should be wise to follow his caution. Look at our missions today. Are there not men who need this caution? Are not the words Christian civilization, Christian education, too often in our mouths? Is there no excuse for men who confound the preaching of Christ with the propagation of this Christian civilization? I suggest that there is: I beg men to consider whether St Paul's argument does not apply to us here also.

(4) And as there was a Christian philosophy in the Church of St Paul's day, so there might be today among our converts. But Christian education does not often for us mean the education which enables a man to speak 'the wisdom of God in a mystery'. We see among our converts sometimes men who can do that, men who can understand and express depths of love in the Cross which we ourselves cannot all fathom. This is a philosophy which penetrates far deeper than the intellect. It embraces the affections, emotions, will and thought, in one whole at one instant, in one word. It is a spiritual apprehension, and is moved by the Holy Spirit given to men. We are sometimes amazed at it; but we do not therefore call the man who can use such expression an educated man. We call him educated or uneducated on quite other grounds. It is his knowledge of the wisdom of the world, which entitles him to be called educated by us.

Is that really as it ought to be? We say that he is a wonderful man but quite uneducated. Is that really the truth? We say that he seems to have a strange understanding of Christ but he is quite too ignorant to lead the church, or to minister her sacraments. Is that spiritually true? Does not such language suggest that we ourselves are really uneducated, and ignorant of that divine philosophy of which St Paul spoke? Knowledge of that philosophy may be the secret of all salvation of body, soul, and spirit. It is not infrequently observed that men who possess it seem to advance far beyond their fellows who know those things which Science teaches, and to reap the fruits which we naturally expect from scientific education. Ideas of social order, of progress, of health, of enlightenment, seem to spring up spontaneously where they appear. I wonder whether this is not inevitable; and whether we are right in assuming that we must preach our social reform on scientific grounds as the only way to its attainment. Perhaps that spiritual wisdom has more power even in the elemental world than we quite understand.

There is then today a scientific education which, as it seems to me, takes exactly that place which philosophy held in St Paul's day, and we do seem to admit exactly what St Paul rejected.

A writer from Japan told us the other day that 'There is a very serious danger of modern Japan trying to adopt Christian moral and social standards without Christ,' and he added: 'We all know what a hopeless, disheartening, disillusioning thing that is; for it is building without foundations.'[1] We do not all know it. The theory that it is the duty of missionaries to do that very thing is widely held and often expressed. We constantly hear our missionaries speak of the importance of 'permeating non-Christian society with Christian ideals', or of 'introducing Christian social conditions' as prior to the conversion of the people to Christ. This is nothing else than saying that Christian ideals, and Christian social conditions are possible for non-Christians; and that there can be Christian ideals apart from Christ, and Christian social conditions apart from Christian faith. Men who practise that teaching are doing precisely what this man calls building without foundations, a thing which he says that we all know to be hopeless.

We drift into this position by stages so gradual and subtle that we scarcely perceive the change. Immersed in educational, medical or social work which we are doing truly for Christ's sake, we call the work Christian; which it is for us because we do it in Christ. Then we transfer this idea to those for whom we work, and we imagine that if it is Christian work in relation to us, it must be Christian work in relation to them: we imagine that the progress which they make must be Christian progress. But for them it is not Christian for they do not make progress as Christians, but as non-Christians. Their progress is not Christian unless they become Christians. So we speak of giving Christian education to non-Christian pupils as if non-Christians could receive Christian education. They could hear Christian teaching, but they cannot receive Christian education unless they become

[1] *World Wide Witness*. The SPG Report for 1922, p. 151.

Christian. If they remain non-Christians they can only assimilate what can be assimilated by non-Christians. They can accept certain teachings of Christ because it is agreeable to their non-Christian thought; but they cannot receive it as Christian. Christian education is education in Christ, and presupposes a certain relationship of the person who receives it to Christ. Eliminate that relationship and the education ceases at once to be Christian for him who receives it. Similarly we speak of Christian healing as though it were Christian for non-Christians; so we speak of Christian social work as if non-Christians could make Christian social progress. In all these cases we transfer to others a relationship which is ours, not theirs. And so we gradually slip into the position of building on another foundation than Christ without being aware of it. It is only in some way such as this I can explain to myself Christian missionaries building as they obviously do, when they put intellectual, moral and social advancement first.

But, however we may explain it, this action certainly does not make for the extension of the Christian Church. It affects us as missionaries. When we put intellectual, moral and social progress first in time we certainly as missionaries become less capable of bringing the people whom we serve to Christ. Immersed in schemes for their improvement, which can be successful as we suppose without being rooted in faith in Christ, we inevitably cease to put their conversion in the first place. The other is first in time: it tends more and more to become first in thought. We become almost content if the people are instructed in our 'Christian ethics' and advance in our 'Christian civilization'; we seem gradually to lose that burning thirst for the conversion of men to Christ which alone seems to equip a man for the work of conversion, or if we do not lose it, we stifle it by listening to those who tell us that civilization and enlightenment are our proper work today and the proper expression of that desire.

Is that statement false or exaggerated? It is certainly exaggerated if we think that it implies that all our missionaries have accepted that position; for they certainly have not; but if it is no more than an assertion that in the missionary body there is a considerable leavening of these ideas, and that a considerable number of missionaries, many of them unconsciously, or in spite of themselves, are affected by them in the way that I have suggested, I am sure that it is neither false nor exaggerated. The ideas are so widespread that they do seriously influence our missionaries and our missionary work as a whole, and influence them in the way which I have said.

Nor does this influence stop with us. Those to whom we go as missionaries instinctively feel that we are relying for progress on those secondary causes which we present to them; that change of circumstances, intellectual education, ethical principles, are the important things; and it is not surprising that they should put their faith in these things; nor that, even if they become Christians, they should follow us in this and put social advancement and intellectual enlightenment in the first place in their thought for the welfare of their country.

It is a fact worthy of note that those converts who are most eager to propagate the faith of Christ, are frequently the men who have received least education at our hands. It is to be expected that it should be so. They are the men who have received from us the faith of Christ as the one source of enlightenment and progress. Christ has been everything to them. They have not learnt to propagate the gospel of social reform, the gospel of enlightenment, or the gospel of sex equality. Social reform is, as we have seen, easily divorced from all religion: enlightenment and civilization are quite compatible with extreme selfishness. It is Christ alone who inspires men with the desire to bring men to Christ. There is nothing in enlightenment and social advancement to compel men to preach Christ. They are more likely, if they have learnt to value our enlightenment, to strive to spread that enlightenment from a desire for the material advancement for their nation, and to combat the encroachment of Europeans upon their liberty.

There is nothing in the gospel of enlightenment to compel men to preach Christ; there is much to hinder them. Spontaneous propagation of the Gospel under these circumstances is hardly to be expected.

Because we find it almost impossible to conceive of any true Christian life under barbarous conditions, or indeed, apart from our 'Christian civilization', and because we are therefore driven to put intellectual and social advance first, we find it almost impossible to admit any spontaneous, native, church expansion. Spontaneous expansion must necessarily be expansion under the material and social conditions of the race. Spontaneous expansion under those conditions means the creation of multitudes of little churches all

94

existing under those conditions. It unquestionably presupposes that the Christian life is possible under those conditions. If, then, we instinctively deny the name of Christian to life under those conditions; if 'Christian life' means for us essentially the kind of civilized life to which we accustomed; if we cannot dissociate the idea of Christianity from the idea of our civilization; if we instinctively seize upon everything which does not seem in harmony with our ideas of civilization to declare that it is 'not Christian'; how can we possibly encourage the spontaneous expansion of the Church? Of course we cannot. We find it more easy to give the name of Christian to a decent civilized life void of Christian faith than to a life devoted to Christ and inspired by Christ under conditions which do not seem to us to be decent. The one we can see, the other we have not eyes to see.

I think any man who would seek the way of spontaneous expansion must face this difficulty; for none of us can deny its reality. Set us face to face with a really barbarous Christianity in Africa for instance, and we should shrink back appalled: most of us, if we were set face to face with Christianity in a different civilization from our own, as for instance in China, would be amazed and confounded, and we should instantly set to work to introduce the familiar civilization which we associate with the idea of Christianity. The way of spontaneous expansion is not easy for such as we are. This does not justify us in rejecting it; neither does it justify us in saying that we are doing everything in our power to encourage it if we have not faced and overcome this difficulty in ourselves.

CHAPTER 7

Missionary Organization

For missionary work we have two organizations; one which is ancient and one which is modern; one simple, the other very cumbrous: the simple necessary organization is the organization of the Church, the cumbrous modern organization is the organization of missionary societies.

The Church was first established and organized with a world-wide mission for a world-wide work. It was a living organism composed of living souls deriving their life from Christ, who was its Head. It was an organism which grew by its own spontaneous activity, the expression of that life which it had in union with Christ, the Saviour. Its organization was the organization fitted for such an organism; it was the organization of a missionary body. Consequently there was no special organization for missions in the Early Church; the church organization sufficed. It was simple and complete. There was abundant room in it for the expression of the spontaneous individual activity of its members; for every member was potentially a missionary; and the Church, as an organized body, expected that activity and knew how to act when its members did their duty. With the activity of its members, it grew simply by multiplying its bishops.

The new modern missionary organization is an addition. With us the Church had largely ceased to be self-expanding: its members had, for the most part, forgotten its missionary character; its organization had degenerated and become stiff and rigid. But the missionary spirit was not dead, and it demanded expression. Naturally, it expressed itself in the form characteristic of a Western people in this age. It took the form of elaborate organization; it created a new organization within the Church. If we compare our modern missionary work with the missionary work of the Early Church, this is what differentiates them: with us missions are the special work of a special organization; in the Early Church missions were not a special work, and there was no special organization.

We can, then, distinguish between the organization of the Church as a missionary body and our modern missionary organization. It is into the nature of this latter organization and its relation to spontaneous expansion that we must now enquire.

The work accomplished by Christian men working in and through this special organization is, without question, the most important that has been done in the world in modern times. No man who believes that ideals are more vital to human progress than material arts, and that spiritual reformation is more necessary for human progress than material improvement, can look out into the world and consider what has been done and the forces which have been set in motion without realizing this. But when we ascribe these results to our modern organization and say, as we often do say, that we have attained these results by our organization, we forget that results as great were attained in the past without our modern organization. The results are due, not to our organization, but to that undying spirit of love for the souls of men which Christ inspires. The modern organization is only the form in which we have expressed that spirit; and a time may come when organization, which seems to us to be absolutely necessary, may cease to be necessary, or may take such different shape as to be hardly recognizable; for it has within it elements of weakness which betray its temporary character.

I

Missionary work is presented to us not as the work of the Church but as the work of private societies within the Church. Our ears are deafened and our hearts hardened by the clamour of competing appeals. Every parish and nearly every individual is bewildered and demoralized by it, as organization strives with organization to gain the ear and touch the pocket of as large a number of people as possible. It is true that a claim is sometimes made on behalf of some society that it 'represents the Church' for missionary work; but if the use of that ambiguous term is meant to suggest that the society which makes the claim has any exclusive or prerogative right to attention, very few people believe it. The mere existence of other societies in the Church for doing similar work disproves it. No society within the Church can have any exclusive right to represent the Church. The Church is, as I have said, in her nature a missionary society; and no group of her members can represent in that sense what she alone is. No society within the Church can be more than an association of individuals for the furtherance of a work in which they are interested. Instinctively men look upon mission work, when presented to them as the special work of societies, as a special interest of a group of Churchmen, a work in which they may or may not take any interest, and may or may not support. No argument shakes that conviction. Missionary work must be either the relation of the Church to the world, or a fad of a few.

II

Missionary organization in these societies is necessarily elaborate. It involves the creation of offices and departments, with directors, clerks, accountants, divided and subdivided. Now elaborate organization exercises a strange fascination over the minds of men; and this is as true of our missionary organization as of any other organization. It tends to become an end in itself. Men incline more and more to rely upon it: they learn to ascribe to it virtues which do not belong to it.

(1) There is a horrible tendency for an organization to grow in importance till it overshadows the end of its existence, and begins to exist for itself. Many men have established organizations in order to achieve by them a definite object, and have been caught in the toils of the organization which they have created. Business men, for instance, have created organizations that by them they might become rich, and then, having grown rich even in their own estimation, have gone on labouring simply to keep the organization in existence. The maintenance of the organization has become a greater incentive to work than the purpose for which it was first created.

This is the truth that Samuel Butler set forth in *Erewhon*, when he depicted men destroying their machines because they were afraid that they might become their slaves, tending and feeding them for their lives. 'May not man himself become a sort of parasite upon the machines; an affectionate, machine-tickling aphid?' 'The servant glides by imperceptible approaches into the master; and we have come to such a pass that, even now, man must suffer terribly on ceasing to benefit the machines.'

The danger is a real one. I heard the other day of an organization started to relieve a certain special evil. It was reported that means might be found to wipe out this evil. The first expression of the directors was not one of joy at such a glorious prospect, but of anxiety for their organization. If this happens, they said, what will become of our organization? and they were quite relieved when they were assured that there would be plenty of work for them to do for many years to come. Suppose that it were indubitably clear that the end for which all these organizations exist would be best served by the elimination of some of them, or by their fusion: would their directors be ready to serve the cause for which the organizations were founded by destroying them? If not, could it be for any other reason than that the organization had become an end in itself apart from the end for which it was created? The directors of each organization would have innumerable arguments to prove that their own organization must be maintained at all costs; and one of the most powerful would be the argument that their subscribers would not support the work except through that particular organization. But is not that to argue that directors and contributors alike put the organization before the work which the organization exists to do? Imagine one of our great missionary organizations losing itself to further the cause for which it exists! Is it credible? But, if it is not, it can only be incredible because we know that organizations have become to no small extent ends in themselves.

(2) Our love of organization leads us to rely upon it. This is not infrequently the cause of failure in the business world. When once an organization has been built up men think that all that is needed is to keep it going and to enlarge it. The direction becomes mechanical, and as the direction becomes mechanical the organization ceases to produce the results expected. This is the cause of much failure in the educational world. Men evolve a method of teaching, and they begin to think that the method can be worked mechanically; and instantly it loses its power. This is still more the case in spiritual work. Yet we hear men talk as if the enlargement of the organization would by itself produce the spiritual results. Give us, they say, so much more money and so many more men and the propagation of the Gospel will advance in proportion. The conclusion is far from certain. That men speak as if it were certain only shows that they are beginning to rely upon the organization to do the work.

(3) Not only does our love of organization lead us to expect from it spiritual results, it also leads us to ascribe to it results which do not belong to it. I have already pointed out a tendency to believe that the great success of our modern missionary work is due to our splendid

organization, while all history shows that success as great, and, perhaps, of a deeper character, has been attained without any such organization as ours. But there is one virtue which we ascribe to our organization which we ought carefully to consider. Men often say that *continuity* in our mission work depends upon our mission organization; and they point to the fact that work supported by an organization like ours does not stop with the death of the man who started it; they point to the fact that some work begun by an individual unsupported by an organization often, apparently, does end with his death.

When we speak of organization securing continuity, we mean that the continuity of the work depends upon the continuity of the organization which supports it. The continuity is really in the organization. If the organization ceases, the work ceases. Some men would, perhaps, go so far as to say that that is precisely what they do mean, as it is certainly what they ought to mean, when they ascribe the continuity of missionary work to our missionary organization. Stop the organization, they would say, and the work will cease.

There is a kind of work which depends for continuity upon the continuity of an organization which supports it; there is also a kind of work which does not. The man who first imported Australian rabbits in tins into England established an organization, and if the organizations which now carry on that work ceased, the continuity of the supply of Australian rabbits to England would cease also. The man who first imported rabbits into Australia was not supported by any organization established to carry on the importation of rabbits. Yet there was no lack of continuity. Muslim expansion in the present day is, as we should say, quite unorganized; yet there is continuity. In these and similar cases continuity depends upon the interior life of that which is propagated. It grows spontaneously by its own inward force, and the continuity consists in the unity of the life.

To insist, then, that our missionary organization is essential for the continuity of that work which we do in foreign lands, and to ascribe the continuity of that work to the organization, is to ascribe to our work a particular character as being in itself lifeless. If the continuity of that work which we do depends upon the organization, it is manifest that the work which we do must be something other than the propagation of life. A human organizaton is necessary to secure the continuity of a human creation; it is not necessary to secure the continuity of that which has life.

But if our work is the propagation of life, if it is to bring men the knowledge of Christ who is life, and who gives men life, then the continuity of the work cannot depend upon a source which cannot give the life but can only minister it; and it cannot be thought to depend upon it, unless those who so think are consciously or unconsciously allowing the organization to usurp Christ's place.

This may be the inward reason why organizations for spiritual work constantly break down. As the organizations grow they assume an undue importance in the minds of their directors and supporters. More and more men begin to rely upon them, more and more they allow them to take that place which is Christ's alone. Then, in order that Christ may be revealed as the only source of life, it is necessary that the organization should manifestly fail, and a great disaster befalls it, which appears to those who are trusting the organization as a disaster to the cause for which the organization was designed. There is a great falling away, a great destruction, a great tribulation, and then, out of the disaster, the tribulation, Christ is revealed once more as the only source of strength, the only Saviour. It may be that the threatening revolt against our missions, to which I have already referred, may usher in such a period of tribulation. The weakness of our organization will be revealed, there will be a great falling away; there will be great destruction and loss; and then Christ will appear once again, and all that is true, all that is rooted in Him, will be made manifest, and will break forth into new life inspired by His undying power.

III

We of today are enamoured of organization; we pride ourselves on our skill in designing and directing it; but when we are dealing with the propagation of the Gospel our love for it leads us into serious dangers. It leads us to give to material an undue importance; it leads us to attempt to organize spiritual forces.

(1) It leads us to give to material an undue importance. That our missionary organization is largely concerned with the collection and administration of material requires little argument. Every report, every magazine issued by any of the societies, reveals it. How anxious this makes our greatest and most spiritual leaders is shown by their constantly repeated warnings. Such men would not say again and

again, we must not allow the material to take the first place in our thoughts, we must not permit the collection of money to distract our attention from the spiritual; unless they knew and felt how real the danger is. The demand for the material is constant, pressing, immediate. It is impossible that men who rely upon voluntary contributions for the support of large and expensive undertakings should not feel the burden; it is almost impossible that this burden should not be often in their thoughts, and often first in their thoughts. It is impossible that their appeals should not emphasize this need and present it to supporters, as it presents itself to them, as the real pressing need of the moment.

Say what they will, strive as they will, the need for material exercises a strong constraint, and thrusts itself continually into the foreground. All our missions have been bound up with the administration of property, the building and equipment of large stations, schools, hospitals, industrial institutions, and the like, all financed largely from home. As years passed the burden grew, and irresistibly the demand for material became more and more insistent, and the collection of funds occupied more and more of our thought and care.

Miss Constance Padwick, speaking of the sudden outbreak of missionary literature for the young in the first half of the nineteenth century, says that 'Examination of the story of the missionary societies during the thirties leads to the conviction that missionary committees had discovered not children but a copper mine.'[1] And a similar examination of the large output of leaflets for missionary intercession, with their persistent emphasis upon appeals for gifts, during the last twenty years, might lead a critical mind to the conviction that their authors had discovered not the power of prayer but a silver mine.

It is difficult to express the sense of overwhelming materialism which a prolonged and careful study of our missionary literature produces upon the mind of the reader. Careful examination reveals very few articles which do not contain, directly or indirectly expressed, an appeal for money. It is 'money' 'money' everywhere, all the time: everything depends upon money. Listen, e.g., to the Bishop of Zanzibar confronted with a possible reduction of £4,500: 'Of course no progress will be possible—no development, no preaching the Gospel in new parts of the diocese,'[2] or to the Bishop of Korea: 'If

[1] *IRM*, Oct. 1917, p. 566
[2] *Ch. Times*, May 25, 1923, p. 595.

the missions of the good old Church of England lag behind those of the American Presbyterians and Wesleyans, it is because they (the latter) have been accorded wealthy support in men and money.'[1]

Abroad we see the same cause producing the same result. The collection of material is the pressing need. The collection of material is an art with which we are familiar. Our methods of collecting funds and of administering them have been carried abroad. There, too, the collection of material is put into prominence and occupies a very large part, not only of our thoughts, but of the thoughts of our native agents and converts. And the claim of the Native Christians, as they grow in knowledge and understanding of the sources of the money, which is now spent in their country to control its use, may lead to serious difficulties. 'About nineteen-twentieths,' we are told on the authority of Dr A. J. Brown, 'of the money now expended on the foreign field comes from Europe and America,' and 'it is,' he says, 'a sound principle that money should be administered by those who are selected by the representatives of the donors and who can be held to accountability for its use.'[2] Moreover, nearly all church property and buildings are held by the Societies.[3] One day, therefore, there may arise no small strife over the administration of this money and the ownership of this property, for, as Dr MacNicol says: 'The power of the purse is in the hands of the foreign missionary, and without that power the Indian leaders feel themselves helpless.'[4] A Chinese writer put it in this form: 'Evangelism in China costs *twelve* million American dollars annually. Towards this immense sum Chinese Christians can contribute *one* million dollars only. This shows that, if Chinese control of the Church means financial independence also, the Chinese Church faces an economic burden it cannot shoulder.' The conclusion is clear: we have taught all our converts to feel helpless without money.

I can imagine that if I were a Muslim the reading of the reports of Christian missionary societies would afford me great satisfaction. I should compare the laborious efforts of the Christians to propagate their religion with the silent spontaneous expansion of Islam. Let them pour out their money, I should say, let them establish all this

---

[1] *Ch. Times*, Oct. 21, 1921, p. 379.
[2] *IRM*, Oct. 1921, p. 486.
[3] This is no longer true—K.G.G.
[4] *IRM*, April 1920, p. 218.

extravagant machinery. They may make a few converts, but they will do us more good than harm. They know not the power of a true religion. Whilst they labour at these material things, we advance by our own inherent spiritual power. They organize and build, they toil and sweat to convert men by their material methods; Islam grows whilst we sit still. With all their gifts they purchase a few converts, and then they must begin all over again in the same costly way to make a few more. One convert to Islam is the sure first fruit of a great harvest. Islam advances automatically. God works without our material aid. These men know nothing of spiritual forces, the forces that work automatically, the power which is of God. I should be wrong; but I should not be wholly wrong. The Christian organization does emphasize the material.

(2) It leads us to attempt to organize spiritual forces. Our love of organization leads us to attempt to fix the place where, and the time at which, and the men by whom, a spiritual movement is to take place. We fix the place. We choose what we call a strategic centre and plant there our buildings and our institutions. There the spiritual movements must take place if we are to be in any way the agents of it. The organization binds us to that place, and there we must stay so long as those buildings stand, and the posts remain open. The society organization demands it. Here is a station; it must be occupied: here is a post vacant; it must be filled. That is quite reasonable if we are dealing with organization for ends which we understand and the means to attain which are more or less in our power; but is a spiritual movement of that character? For spiritual work spiritual organization is necessary; but can we create a spiritual organization of spiritual forces? Only a divine intelligence can do that. But we attempt to do the work of that divine intelligence; by fixing our stations and immobilizing our men. Consequently, we see spiritual movements taking place not far from us, and we ourselves outside them, or, if not outside them altogether, utterly incapable of taking our proper part in them. What we can do is to organize our own powers, and that we do within the limits of our intelligence. We can organize the external arrangements of a church, the provision of its ministers and ornaments and buildings, and we can train men for that organization. But to be God's agents in spiritual movements we must follow, not lead. We want to lead, and, trying to lead, we are simply left behind. We say: 'Here we will have our buildings,' but

the spiritual movements may be growing unseen by us in another place and by other means.

We fix the time. We say: 'Now we will organize a spiritual advance.' We tried to do that in the war by a National Mission. Others all over the world have tried, and are trying, to do the like. But they do not know the time, and the time does not come at the bidding of the organization. While the organization is cumbrously labouring, the time is at hand, and come, and passing away, and the organization has nothing, or little, to do with it. The organization is always too late. For we can organize the external results of a spiritual movement, but we cannot organize a spiritual movement.

We fix the persons. We can create posts and select men to fill them; but we cannot choose the persons through whom spiritual movements are to take place. We in a dim way recognize a spiritual person when we see him, but to fill our posts we have to take the best men whom we can get. We have to fill the posts at all costs, somehow, if we possibly can. Therefore the administrators of the organization choose as well as they can and hope for the best. But it is not possible in that way to choose men to be agents of a spiritual movement. The true agents may be other men in quite other positions than our posts.

We know that well enough; but, nevertheless, the organization of missions, being an organization *for* a spiritual work, only too often becomes in our eyes the organization *of* a spiritual work. It is only too easy to slip from that '*for*' to that '*of*' and we do it constantly. In all our selection of strategic points ,as we call them, in all our creation of institutions, in all our talk of 'forward movements', we are constantly on the verge of this offence, of speaking and thinking as if we could organize spiritual forces.

IV

Our organization immobilizes our missionaries. It creates and maintains large stations and great institutions, and these absorb a very great proportion of our energy. We cannot move freely. A mission station is indeed a contradiction in terms: mission implies movement, station implies stopping. This modern term has a strange significance. The maintenance and direction of great schools, hospitals, and churches with their innumerable guilds and societies confine our activity within narrow limits. When once these things have been established the missionaries who established them must stay to look after them, and any advance must be made by others. Nay more, when for some cause the missionaries in charge of these institutions fail in numbers, men engaged in opening new work must be recalled to direct the institutions. The larger they are, the more expensive, the more elaborate, the more they demand the first care of the missionaries. Any other work must be laid aside that these may be maintained. Great opportunities, widespread movements towards Christ, must be neglected rather than that these institutions should lack workers. The immobilized force must be maintained at all costs, the mobile must wait for recruits. How many missions have any mobile force at all?

Similarly, we immobilized native evangelists. We found a man who showed some evangelistic zeal, we brought him into our system, we trained him and paid him, and then fixed him in a definite spot as a teacher or catechist. He could no longer move freely from village to village appealing to those whose hearts God touched: he was compelled to stay year after year in a place where often his message was becoming year after year less effective, holding, in our phraseology, a lonely and difficult outpost. And then when he broke down we were grieved and disappointed, or even angry, with him.

v

In our organization missionaries are a professional class. Christians leave our shores in great numbers: few are, or think themselves to be or think that they ought to be, missionaries of the Gospel. We do not expect that where they go the heathen will be converted and churches established spontaneously. It is almost universally taken for granted that missionary work is the work of a paid professional class, and that the utmost that can be expected of those who do not belong to this class is to support those who do; and even that is not expected of the majority. Missionary societies began their crusade, not by striving to call out the spirit of Christian men whose occupation carried them abroad, not by trying to impress upon the Church at home that Christ calls *all* His people to witness for Him wherever they may be, wherever they may go, but by creating an army of professional missionaries. The whole system of societies, boards, offices, accounts, contracts with missionaries, statistical returns, reports, reeks of it. From every missionary society there goes out every day and all day into every part of the world with one insistent unceasing voice the proclamation that the Gospel must be preached in all the world, and that it must be preached by special agents maintained by a society for this particular work. No verbal denials can shake it.

We created this paid professional missionary class not to support spontaneous missionary zeal on the part of our fellow countrymen, but to take the place of it: in the same way we created a paid professional class of mission agents among our converts not to support spontaneous expression of missionary zeal, for we did not dream of it, but to take the place of it. We were persuaded that to carry on the work in the country we must have paid professional native agents. It is one of the most wonderful and amazing things in our modern religious thought that we have carried everywhere all over the world our stipendiary system as if it were an essential part of the Gospel which we preach. We were convinced that we must see to it that every little group of converts was in the care of some catechist or teacher, and that we must find evangelists to preach in the country and that they must all be paid agents. The need for workers was pressing. Naturally we seized upon every man who showed any zeal or ability, and we encouraged boys in mission schools, who showed any promise, to seek employment in the mission.

Mr Hibbert Ware, writing of the boarding schools connected with the Telugu Mission in 1915, says:

> All these were brought into existence solely for this purpose, and although other boys, by paying their own fees, may receive their education in them, yet they are still kept up entirely with the view of supplying the Mission's annual demand for agents. At a certain stage of their course, not very advanced, every one has to face the question whether he is prepared to pledge himself to serve the Mission, when his time is completed, for a definite period of about seven years. If he is not, he must resign his scholarship, which is intended solely to train a student for mission work. Practically all the boys look forward, from the time they first enter a boarding school to mission service.[1]

There grew up a regularly ordered system. Mission workers were classed, and paid according to their class, just like government clerks. The basis of classification was pay, and zealous work was rewarded with an advance in position and a corresponding increase in salary.

[1] *The East and the West*, April 1915, p. 207.

Mission agents brought up under such a system as this are liable to four very serious temptations.

(1) They are tempted to think an increase of pay the one test of progress. If, at the end of a reasonable time, a man does not obtain the status and pay of a higher class it argues that his conduct has been not quite what it ought to have been. I once came across a striking illustration of this in India. A poor destitute cripple educated at the expense of a missionary, made remarkable progress, and developed great spiritual powers, and exercised a wonderful influence over those with whom he came in contact. Seeing this the missionary made him a reader in a leper asylum, where he could drag himself about from house to house and teach the inmates. All went well for a year or two: then he sent in an application for the pay of a higher class. This greatly disturbed his benefactors. 'Here,' they said, 'is a man who has received everything from us and we thought he was working from pure love of Christ, yet the first use that he makes of his new powers is to demand a salary.' It is not necessary to conclude that he was not really working for love of Christ. Salary was a part of the system in which he lived. The only symbol of progress was an increase of pay. In his own eyes and in the eyes of his fellows, to fail to receive the higher position and the higher pay would have been proof that in some way he had not done his duty.

(2) They are tempted to a low conception of their work. They are paid by the mission, they are tempted to work for the mission. It is almost universally confessed that our converts look upon the work of the mission as our work. Mission agents are men paid to take part in our work. So long as they look upon it as our work only men of exceptional spiritual character will be able to look upon it as Divine work. So long as they are servants of the mission only men of rare spiritual character will be able to rise above the idea of their service which that title suggests. And the heathen round them (and it is very important what the heathen think) will be quite unable to see anything more.

(3) There is great temptation to servility of mind and practice. It is curious how often our missionaries find dependence and timidity characteristic of their mission workers. But the system tends to exaggerate any such weakness. It is always safe for the mission agent to wait for instructions. He is separated from his own people by religion, from his congregation by education, from his superior

officer by race. He stands in a peculiarly isolated position. If he appeals for a command there will be no hesitation in giving it on the part of the foreigner, and, right or wrong, no risk in obeying it on his part. Independent action, on the other hand, is always risky. To practise independence under such circumstances demands almost superhuman strength of character.

(4) Not unnaturally there is among mission agents much discontent. In the early days of a mission in country districts the position of the native agent is not unenviable. He is better educated than his fellows and he is guarded against the terrors of absolute destitution. But the moment that other Christians attain to the same position of security by secular occupations they tend to despise mission agents as men who earn small salaries by serving the mission. The more the congregation advances in secular education and wealth, the stronger this tendency becomes, with the result that the better and more capable of the younger generation refuse to accept this service.

Such a service must breed discontent among those who accept it. They blame their own people, they blame the missionaries. They constantly complain that the missionaries do not associate with them on equal terms, that they treat them as servants, that young men from England are set over experienced natives. And for the sake of their own self-respect they naturally covet the status and salaries of European missionaries. There is a divine discontent, and there is a discontent which is far from divine. The temptation which besets the mission agent is a temptation to a discontent which drags down the soul, not to the discontent which spurs it on.

To what a height this professional view of missionary work has grown may be seen from a sentence written by the Editor of *The East and the West* in January 1921. 'If we remove a pecuniary grievance,' he says, 'it would go far towards securing for the service of the Christian Church many of the best educated Indians who are at present to be found in Government employ.' This is no exceptional statement: something of the kind occurs frequently in missionary reports and speeches: it expresses only a common thought; but it contains the pure doctrine of professionalism. The service of the Church is set over against government employment: Christian men do not serve the Church except in the service of the Church, that is as paid professionals: the inducement to enter the service of the Church is the same as the inducement to serve the Government, that is pecuniary profit.

VI

This system thus rooted in the material and the professional is something essentially 'of' us; it springs from us, it expresses our spirit. Everybody knows that we established it because it was suited to us and our work. Here in the West it is at home; anywhere else it is foreign in the innermost sense of that word. How foreign it is becomes at once apparent if we consider the difficulties which arise when we try to find terms on which men of another race can be admitted to those higher offices which we have hitherto held ourselves. We are constantly being told that the organization can only be efficiently worked by foreign directors. Nearly all our missionaries seem to be agreed that very few natives can carry on our organization. Foreigner succeeds foreigner in the direction of nearly all our missionary work; and when any advance is to be made, the first cry is for an increase in the number of foreign directors. A century of teaching, a multitude of converts, make, comparatively speaking, little difference: the organization remains, what it always was, ours, something which we alone can direct and use. For the natives of the country, with a few rare exceptions, it remains an organization which can only admit them to subordinate positions, while the great mass of native Christians can find no proper place in it. If they can be said to be organized at all for missionary work, it is only in as far as they can assist the foreign missionary, follow his directions, or support the work by their contributions. So far from assisting them to propagate the Gospel, the organization positively hinders them; because they cannot understand or use it for themselves.

It is not surprising that the ablest native Christians decline to join such an organization. It is not really pecuniary loss which keeps them from mission work. Able young men in England join the ranks of the missionaries paid by a society because they understand the organization, and can find in it full scope for their powers; but they would soon cease to offer themselves, if they found that they must work all their lives under a foreigner directing a system foreign to them. It is really not true to say that the native Christians decline mission work because they want larger salaries than missions can afford to give: it is much more true that they decline because they cannot endure to spend all their lives in subordination to a foreigner directing a foreign system in which the power of the purse is the prevailing force, and money the thing of the first importance. Thus our materialism and professionalism has ended in driving many of the best men away from missionary work.

VII

Contrast with that the power of voluntary unpaid service. In an article on India's Mass Movements in the *International Review of Missions* for April 1917, Dr Warne says:

> In the Hindustani speaking country there is in each caste community in each village a headman who is called a *chaudhri*. The *chaudhris* have long been the representatives of their communities as non-Christians, and on becoming Christians we take them over as leaders if they are suitable men, if not, the Christians elect other men. . . . We could have had a *chaudhri* movement much sooner but we made the mistake of thinking that such poor people should be paid for service, and we gave the *chaudhris* who worked part of their time a small salary. This did two things: it changed the work from the realm of voluntary to paid service, and it limited the number of workers to those who received part salary. Since *chaudhri* work has been made voluntary, . . . voluntary workers are counted not by hundreds but by thousands. . . .
>
> A paid Indian preacher, be he ever so good, has little authority and power over the social life of a village Christian community as compared to the *chaudhri*. Our experience is that when the responsibility for the social and religious life and the instruction of his community has been taken over by the *chaudhri*, he works at the problem and from a new point of view welcomes the help of the preacher.[1]

If a missionary organization ought to assist the evangelization of the world, when it is apparent that the great majority of the Christians, living in the midst of vast heathen populations, cannot use the organization which we have set up without foreign assistance, and the few who think that they can are driven into opposition, the only conclusion is that the work cannot be done through that organization. Many years ago an African educated in Western schools compared our attempts to propagate Christianity with the attempt of the Romans to introduce Roman civilization into Britain. The comparison is painfully apt. Roman civilization flourished for a time where Roman influence was strong, but the natives never

[1] *IRM*, April 1917, pp. 204, 205.

really understood it; and when the Romans withdrew it passed away with them.

VIII

Canon Gairdner, of Cairo, has warned us against 'missions by proxy', and has suggested that there is a terrible danger that we shall beget native communities in our own likeness, who will also insist before long on doing their work by proxy.[1] He might have gone further. We have created and are creating, and must create, such communities because we carry everywhere the stipendiary system on which the work of our Societies is based and teach all our converts that it is the duty of Christians to evangelize by paying evangelists. Our missionary organization is essentially organization of missions by proxy.

Within such a professional system as ours there can be little room for spontaneous activity. All men naturally tend to leave direct missionary work to a professional class when there exists a professional class whose special duty it is to do it. They inevitably tend to turn to that class and to the societies which support it, and to appeal to them rather than to begin themselves to do what they see needs to be done. The existence of the societies and the professional class seems to relieve all but a few of the most active and earnest of their responsibility: it affords all but the most zealous an excuse for inactivity.

A professional class does not easily encourage the spontaneous zeal of men who are not members of their profession. Spontaneous activity is indeed rather alarming to those who direct an organization such as ours. When the propagation of the faith is spontaneous, and each expresses his own zeal in his own way, not the saint alone, but the charlatan, may find an opportunity for acquiring an influence over others. Side by side with St Peter is Simon Magus; side by side with Demetrius is Diotrephes. In the working of an organization the man who is welcome, the man who is at home, is the plain, mechanical, orderly man who will keep within the bounds. Not only the swindler, but the inspired saint is a difficulty. He appears self-willed, extravagant, eccentric. He is independent, and is always on the verge of breaking the orderly methods of the organization. Our organization tends always to keep the mean. If it checks the exuber-

[1] *Brotherhood, Islam's and Christ's*, p. 20.

ance of genius, if it checks the inspired saint, it checks also the charlatan. Consequently, it seems to many minds safe. In word we often say that we wish that all the Lord's people were prophets, but we generally mean that we wish they would all work diligently in and for the organization, under the direction of those responsible for the organization.

IX

This form of organization is natural to men with our character and experience: it is not in any sense a universal mode of expression. The erection of buildings, the management of property and the creation of an army of professional preachers is to us at this moment of the world's history the natural and obvious method of carrying on our work. This kind of organization suits our capacities, appeals to our sense of fitness, satisfies our eyes. But an elaborate material machinery for the propagation of ideas seems to most of those to whom we go almost absurd. You do not want buildings and machinery to propagate ideas or a faith: you want ideas and a faith. Organization and buildings ought to follow and spring out of the working of the ideas and the faith. Our organization seems to them to put the wrong things first. We collect money and pay men to preach and teach. Outside our circle nearly all men think that very strange. All knowledge, above all, religious knowledge, is a divine gift and to connect it with money is a sort of simony. A paid preacher is suspected as a preacher paid to teach what he is told to teach by those who pay him; not the inspired possessor of a divine gift.

An organization which collects money and pays salaries to missionaries of a divine faith seems to such men a monstrous thing, wholly unspiritual. If those who direct it expect to propagate a faith by building preaching rooms and schools and hospitals, they show that they have no idea what spiritual forces are, or how they work. It is true that a certain number of our converts, by long association with us, learn to shake off these ideas, and that some non-Christians imitate us in this as in other Western practices; but the vast majority never understand our organization: it is to them foreign in the innermost sense of that word.

X

Nor are the religious ideas which render our organization obnoxious to others wholly unknown among ourselves. Even within our own circle the same thought is at work. Many men at home admit it, and their attitude towards the preaching betrays their thought. They know that many preachers who receive salaries are the possessors of a divine gift; but for the preaching of paid preachers as a body they have little respect. They give quite a different kind of attention to a man whom they know to be preaching simply because he cannot help saying what is in his heart. Even to some of us an organization which exists to provide buildings and salaries for men who would never preach unless training and salaries had been provided for them seems to be treading a dangerous path. A day may not be far off when even at home the organization which we now carry abroad will undergo radical change.

For such a change the missionary societies have themselves prepared the way. Their preachers have taught us from every pulpit that the Church ought to be a missionary body. They have reiterated the command of Christ: they have almost exhausted argument to convince us that expansion is for the Church the law of life. It is not then surprising that men, seeing the chaotic state of our missionary organization, and groaning under its innumerable appeals, should begin to demand that the Church be her own missionary society. That demand must issue in a reconsideration of the nature of the Church and of her organization in relation to missions, and the discovery that her organization is in its essential characteristics the organization of a missionary body.

Again, the societies have taught us from every pulpit that every Christian should be at heart a missionary, on the unshakable ground that the spirit of Christ is given to all Christians, and that the spirit given is the spirit which longs for and strives after the salvation of all men in Christ. That teaching has not been without effect. Many are beginning to believe it, and one day many will act on it. The preacher, no doubt, expected a reaction in the form of support for his society, and no doubt it generally took that form, but there is no reason why it should take that form. There is nothing in the teaching to convince anyone that to express his missionary zeal he need support, or belong to, any other society than the Church to which he already belongs. It is not necessary, though it may be convenient, to support any special society in order to do missionary work.

Not every man is able to express his missionary zeal best by joining any of these special organizations. He may not want to become the agent of any of these societies. If the Church is a missionary society and he a churchman, he may well feel that the society of which he is a member suffices. He may well prefer the larger society, unless he needs the support of the smaller society. If he wants that, he must of course conform to the orders and methods of the society of which he becomes an agent. But if he does not want that help, he is doing nothing disorderly in acting freely. He does not cease to be a Christian and a member of a missionary body because he does not add to the order of the Church the more elaborate and precise order of some society organization. The only reason why men have not so acted more often is because they have been obsessed with the idea that a man to express his missionary zeal properly must be a member of some other body within the Church and that church membership is not sufficient.

Many before now have thought that if they were to express their zeal freely outside the limits and restrictions of a special missionary society, they must go outside the Church itself. But that is absurd. The multiplication of societies, which, viewed as a missionary organization for the attainment of a common object, is wasteful, has at least kept before us the truth that men can work outside the societies without working outside the Church. Men disliked the societies in existence, or they wanted some special work done which the societies were not doing, and they did not hesitate to act outside the then existing societies. It never occurred to them to think that in so doing they were violating any church order in founding a new association. But what a group of men can do without violating church order, any individual can do. Canon Gairdner, in the paper which I quoted above, points out the urgent need for their multiplication. He pleads for unofficial missionaries.[1] The organized societies would call such men free lances; but free lances from the point of view of the societies are not free lances from the point of view of the Church: they are simply members of the Church who are doing their duty to Christ and the Church. They are noble examples to all indolent and slothful members. They are men who prefer the apostolic order and method to the modern elaboration. If they multiplied in number it would speedily be found that the church organization was wide enough to embrace their work.

It is commonly supposed that such action would lead to chaos. So

[1] *Brotherhood, Islam's and Christ's*, p. 21.

far from leading to chaos it would lead to order. The organization which is really the source of all order in the Church would assume its proper and rightful place. Church organization would take the place now occupied in most men's minds by missionary organization. The societies would then appear to be what they really are, associations of Christian men designed to assist certain workers and certain kinds of work within the Church. They would occupy in relation to the Church a position somewhat like that which rich philanthropists occupy in relation to society when they provide funds for the establishment of scholarships and fellowships, or of colleges or libraries, or other useful institutions.

This argument applies not only to us but to our converts abroad. They too have been restrained by the confusion of missionary organization with church organization; they too have been taught that if they work outside the missionary organization they work outside the Church. With them this restraint has been far more severe than it has been with us, because the missionaries have represented to them both the society organization and church organization. But already in the mission field a distinction is being made, and churches are transferred from the 'missionary organization' to the 'church organization'. By degrees the Christians will realize the importance of that distinction; and if we teach them what we teach at home, that every Christian in virtue of his reception of Christ's spirit should be a missionary, we may expect them one day to arrive at the inevitable conclusion that there is no need for a man to add any other organization to the church organization in order to exercise his right to teach others, and they may arrive at this conclusion more easily than we ourselves, because they have not that innate delight in elaborate organization which is peculiarly our own.

But that can only be if church organization becomes once more, what it originally was, an organization in which the free, unfetttered zeal of Christian men is recognized and consolidated.

CHAPTER 8

Ecclesiastical Organization

I said at the beginning of my last chapter that we have two organizations for missionary work, one modern, the missionary society, and the other ancient, the Church. But when we consider the organization of the Church today as an organization for missionary work, we must not expect to find it unimpaired in its original purity. In the beginning the Church was a missionary society: it added to its numbers mainly by the life and speech of its members attracting to it those who were outside. Where they went churches were organized, where they settled, men who had never heard of the Church saw the Church, and, being attracted by the life, or by the speech, of its members, learned its secret, joined it, and were welcomed into it. Today members of the Church are scattered all over the world, but they do not carry the Church with them in their own persons, they were not organized, they very often do not desire the conversion of those among whom they live, they do not welcome them into the Church. So societies are formed to do this for them. The Church, as a Church, is not a missionary society enlarging its borders by multiplying local churches; so societies are formed within it to do its work for it. Obviously they cannot do it properly.

We may compare the relation of the societies to the Church with the institution of divorce in relation to marriage. Just as divorce was permitted for the hardness of men's hearts because they were unable to observe the divine institution of marriage in its original perfection, so the organization of missionary societies was permitted for the hardness of our hearts, because we had lost the power to appreciate and to use the divine organization of the Church in its simplicity for the purpose for which it was first created. And just as men could never have recovered the divine perfection of the first institution simply by making divorce illegal; because the perfection of the divine institution did not depend on the legality or illegality of divorce, but upon a divine conception of the relationship of human beings one with another; so the divine perfection of the Church as a missionary society cannot be recovered simply by abolishing the missionary societies, and saying, Let the Church be her own missionary society.

That is not enough. We often hear men say that, and talk as if that would suffice: we see it practised; and the result is, not the organization of the groups of churchmen all over the world as churches, but the creation of a Board of Missions for the Church which is nothing more than a department of church organization, and is in its spiritual character almost identical with a missionary society within the Church. Just as the divine perfection of the institution of marriage could only be recovered by such an understanding of the divine Will for men and such a union of human beings in God as would make the suggestion of divorce monstrous and a law permitting it ridiculous, so the missionary perfection of the Church can only be recovered by such an apprehension of the divine purpose of her creation, and such an understanding of her organization as essentially missionary, that the suggestion of the creation of a missionary society or of a department within her for the prosecution of missionary work would appear ridiculous to the point of absurdity. Divorce was permitted because men's conception of marriage and their use of it were far from that which was in the beginning; missionary societies, and missionary boards are permitted because men's conception of the Church and their use of her organization are far removed from that which was in the beginning.

Nevertheless, though divorce was allowed for the hardness of men's hearts, still the divine perfection of the first institution was man's proper heritage, and is to be recovered in Christ, and so the divine institution of the Christian Church as a missionary society is the proper heritage of churchmen and we may yet recover it; but at the moment we must confess that we have it not. We should see it restored tomorrow in the mission field, if only we would establish churches there today.

I

In my last chapter I pointed out that the modern missionary societies began their work not by recalling the Church to the reality of her own character but by attempting to do her missionary work for her. Consequently in this attempt they naturally organized their work in their own way. They established mission stations, and created a host of lay agents, catechists and teachers and evangelists, to preach in the villages round the stations, to teach inquirers and converts, and to lead the congregations. These were at first all paid agents of the missionary society, and they were trained under the direction of missionaries in mission schools and worked under the direction of missionary superintendents, or of councils which the missionaries created and controlled. There was thus in the mission field an organization of the Christians under the societies, which could be easily distinguished from the Church.

But the societies proclaimed that they sent out their agents as representing the Church, and they desired to found native churches in the countries to which they went. This they could not do. Only a church could propagate itself, and beget churches. The societies realized that their agents could not ordain native clergy; they could only create orders of lay workers. A bishop was necessary for the establishment of a church. They appealed therefore for missionary bishops; and slowly and hesitatingly bishops were appointed to organize churches in the mission field.

The conception of the Church, held both by the episcopacy at home and by the leaders of the societies, was identical. They were far removed from the Apostolic Church: the only church organization with which they were familiar was the organization of a national church, in a country which had for centuries been nominally Christian. They thought of bishops as great officials governing and directing, more or less, large numbers of clergy, most of whom they scarcely knew by sight, in dioceses so large that they could not possibly visit the parishes except at rare intervals. They thought of parish priests as officials of the Church who ruled almost autocratically in their parishes, responsible not at all to the laity for their conduct, and only partially to their bishops. They thought of the laity not so much as members of the Church as people whose duty it was to obey the Church as represented by her bishops and priests. The apostolic conception of the bishop as the father of a spiritual family, as the pastor of a flock every member of which he should know by name, was lost. Men still used the titles 'Chief Pastor' and 'Father in God'; but they did not expect him to know his family, or his flock, personally and intimately. Both bishop and priest were officials, and paid officials, separated widely from the laity by training and by conventional manners and customs.

It was the organization of this stationary national Church which we attempted to apply to the mission field. By dint of diligent and persevering collection, sufficient money was secured to endow bishoprics with a stipend which the authorities considered adequate, and bishoprics were established. Some huge portion of the earth's surface was marked off in which a mission or missions existed, and that was called a diocese. So a bishop was given six provinces of China as a diocese, when he was the leader of a band of half-a-dozen missionaries with two or three mission stations in two of the provinces. A country the size of Germany was thought a proper diocese for a single bishop. The head missionary at a mission station was similarly called a parish priest, and he called a mission district the size of Wales or Yorkshire his parish, though he had not, and probably never would, set foot in large parts of it.

Obviously this church organization corresponded sufficiently well to the missionary organization. The bishop appointed was generally a missionary, or heartily in sympathy with the work of the societies, and the societies generally subscribed a considerable part of the endowment of the See. He knew as much of the work done by his clergy in his diocese as most of the English bishops knew of theirs. The superintending missionaries in idea corresponded sufficiently closely to the parish priests at home, and the other clergy, native or foreign, to curates at home. The district was looked upon as a parish, the church buildings of the little congregations in it corresponded more or less to church buildings in parishes in England. The fact that an organization in which the parish priest lived within a few miles of his most distant parishioners was being applied to an area in which he was removed from the majority of them by a journey of days or weeks was overlooked: the system nominally applied. There was a bishop, there were priests, there was a laity. What more could anyone ask? If we imagine St Paul being solemnly appointed bishop of Europe, or St Mark as parish-priest of Galatia; if we think of St Mark travelling up and down seventy miles round Antioch in Pisidia to administer the sacraments, and of the churches of Italy and Greece dependent for confirmations upon St Paul; if we think of St Paul sending urgent appeals to Antioch for a priest for Rome or Corinth, as we appeal for Benares or Peking; we see at once the difference between the apostolic organization of the Church and the organization which we exported from England.

The bishops, then, sent from England, established this type of church organization, but the organization of the native Christians under the missionary societies in many parts of the world did not therefore cease. One society might proclaim itself the mere hand-maid of the Church and desire that all its work should be directed by the bishop; but another might claim to direct its own missionary operations in its own way. Where this was the case difficulties inevitably arose, for there were in fact two ecclesiastical organizations in the same place. Very early the bishop began to argue that the evangelization of the country was the duty of the Church in the country; and as representing the Church he claimed to direct the missionary policy of the societies. I have myself heard bishops complain that a society allowed and encouraged its agents to establish stations in places within his diocese so far distant that he could not possibly supervise their work. This was the inevitable result of our church organization which created vast dioceses in which a bishop was lost, instead of creating bishops wherever there were Christians to form a church. Instead of rejoicing that a new church was springing into existence in a far distant part of the country the bishop was reduced to complaining of such a misfortune. This action, however unhappy, brought into sharp relief the fact that the mission was not the Church. There was a certain rivalry between the bishop as representing church organization and the secretaries of societies as representing the society organization.

The delegates sent out to India by the Church Missionary Society in 1921 recognized what a serious difficulty this was. They said:

> The outstanding fact in our present Church Missionary Society administration is that in the great majority of the dioceses it is quite outside diocesan control. . . . It is impossible for such an organization to be other that a divisive influence in the diocese, for as an inevitable result there are two authorities, on the one hand the bishop and his office and his councils, on the other hand the Church Missionary Society secretary and his office and his committees, and the more strong and efficient the Church Missionary Society secretary, his office, and his committees, the more divisive will be their influence. . . . It will be obvious that when the dioceses are controlled by Indian bishops, as in many cases they will be with the coming extension of the episcopate, the cleavage indicated and the antagonism resulting will be even more apparent.[1]

[1] Report of the CMS Delegation to India, 1921–1922, p. 30

II

One very prominent feature of missionary organization was the establishment of committees of missionaries in which questions of policy and finance were considered, and when the missionaries began to talk of the establishment of a native church they naturally thought first of councils. It was largely by their action that church councils for districts or larger areas were established, and these councils were recognized as part of the diocesan organization, that is, of the church organization as opposed to the missionary organization.

These councils were certainly a great advance on the pure autocracy of foreign missionaries, but they still further misled the native Christians as to the true character of church organization. As I have already pointed out[1] the great multitude of the converts lived in congregations which were not churches, and when church councils were put into the prominent place while the fundamental simplicities were neglected, they did not find the church which they joined a little family in the town or village guided by a father, a bishop who knew every one of them intimately, a family in which all were mutually responsible for the well-being of the whole; they did not find it a school in which all together were learning to grow in grace under the guidance of their most experienced and respected elders; they learned that it was a strange form of government in which they might elect a representative to attend a council to do something which they did not understand, generally with the result that they were asked to increase their contributions; while far away there was an exalted ruler called a bishop from whom they might occasionally receive a visit. That the conception of church organization which the native Christians have learned is the conception of an arrangement of councils to control the finances and policy of a body consisting of a multitude of congregations which are not churches only makes confusion worse confounded.

Over these church councils the missionaries had at first, and still have generally, complete control; and though, as I have said, these councils were not really part of the missionary organization, little friction arose. But as intellectual education spread among the native Christians, they began to appreciate the powers of a council in finance and administration, and they naturally fixed upon the coun-

[1] Chapter 3.

122

cil as the important element in church organization, and saw that if they could dominate the church councils they could gain control over the affairs of the district, or of the whole diocese. Nay more, just as in early days bishops had claimed, as representing the Church, to control the policy of missionary societies, so now, in the more advanced areas, the native Christians in councils, as representing the Church, inevitably claim the right to control the policy and finances of the foreign missionary societies working in their country. Hence has arisen the struggle which we now see going on between the Church, as represented by the more intellectual and wealthy Christians, and the Mission. It is essentially a struggle first to free the Church from missionary control, and then to control the Mission by subordinating it to the Church as represented by the church councils. Today the question which absorbs almost more attention than the conversion of the heathen is the question of the relation of Church and Mission; how much authority the Mission must resign, how much it can safely retain in its own hands. The Church Missionary Society delegates to India did not conceal their anxiety: 'It is not too much to say that unless some definite steps are taken to withdraw the control which the society still exercises over the congregations and churches there will be dangerous embitterment, and probably schisms in various places.[1] This is true not only of India, but of many other parts of the mission field; and it will soon be true of all; for everywhere like causes will sooner or later produce like results.

The last stage of the controversy is at hand in India where the Church Missionary Society proposes 'to take in hand forthwith the transfer of the whole of its work from the Society to the dioceses' with the significant reservations: 'It is inherent in the situation that the supporters of a society in the West must believe in its work if they are to continue their support. Inevitably grants must cease if their sympathy is forfeited.' And: 'We propose that the diocesan bodies controlling the Society's work should be constituted on an elective basis. This can be so arranged as to secure the inclusion of a due representation of the Society's missionaries, and also of Indian representatives of those districts in which the Society has been responsible for the instruction of the Church for many years past.'

It is difficult to believe that any such scheme which needs such safeguards can be more than a mere palliative, an expedient which

[1] Report of the CMS Delegation to India, 1921–1922, p. 18.

may or may not tide over a period of difficult transition; but the time cannot be very far distant when the native Church as represented by its bishops and its councils will insist on being master in its own house, whatever may happen to grants made by a society in the West.

III

But in many parts of the world, seeing the difficulties which two ecclesiastical organizations created, we made great efforts really to identify the Mission and the Church. We began by sending a bishop as head of the Mission. There was in theory only one organization and that church organization; but unfortunately it was church organization of that type which I have already described. Like Nebuchadnezzar's image, its head was of gold, its belly of brass, and its feet part of iron and part of clay. It stood upon feet of iron and clay, paid lay workers, and congregations which were not churches; its head was high uplifted, one solitary potentate, the bishop; and between these there was an utterly inadequate number of priests, quite unable to provide nourishment for the whole; but strong and exclusive as brass.

Moreover, in practice it was impossible to identify the Mission with the Church. Theoretically the Church and the Mission were one; but it was impossible for most of the missionaries to identify themselves with the natives in the Church. We habitually speak of the native Church as something distinct from the Mission. We habitually speak of the Mission as something which is to pass, and the Church as something which is to survive and remain when the Mission is withdrawn. The native Christians also inevitably make a distinction between the Mission and the Church. The Mission consists of missionaries assisted by a number of natives whom they select and train to help them in their work; but they are essentially not of the country, and are liable to retire at any moment to a distant land when sickness or other calls make it desirable.

We cannot but recognize that everywhere we have established missions, and missions are not churches. The early Church sent out missionaries, but it established no missions: we establish a mission and give it a certain permanence whilst yet we always speak of it as something passing. The consequence is that we get at once a confusion of thought and a conflict of action. The mission is to establish the church; but it establishes itself, and exists over against the church. This is not Biblical. It is not really a question, as we nearly always say, of times and circumstances, of race and age, it is a question of principle and spirit. If we establish missions instead of establishing churches it is because we differ from the apostles and the early Church in principle and in spirit. I do not want to labour this point, I only want to suggest that so profound a difference in action cannot be the effect of mere change of circumstances.

Seeing then that over the whole mission field the native church can be distinguished from the mission in this respect, that everywhere the mission proclaims its passing character, and seeing that the mission can never cover the field; and that that work must be the work of the native church, we have everywhere set ourselves to prepare natives to take over those positions which the foreigners of the mission now occupy, and we have taught them to look forward to a day when the native church will be directed by its own priests and bishops. The problem of Church and Mission is really the same in character everywhere.

IV

When we turn to consider how we attempt to bring this to pass, obviously we shall find that our attempt is conformed to that conception of the Church and her organization which is carried abroad with us. Everywhere the cry today is that the mission must train leaders for the native church to be. What this preparation is I find expressed very clearly in an article in *The East and the West* for April 1909. It was written by Bishop King, who was then Bishop in Madagascar, and has since been General Secretary of the SPG. His paper represents the attitude of the official of the Church on the mission field and the official of the society at home; and describes a training which is familiar to all who are acquainted with our work abroad; for it is a training still followed everywhere almost universally. In this article he distinguishes five steps in the path by which a native ministry is to be reached:

(1) The foreign missionary begins to fasten on certain of his scholars and consciously to train them for future work. Why does he do this? Because he grows fond of his best pupils and tries to keep them near him. The majority of those whom he teaches are clearly incapable of receiving a good education: they are good fellows, but they are stupid; but there

are some three or four pupils whose intelligence is of a higher order, and whom he hopes to educate and to use. In acting thus he is naturally led to the only possible path of development in his work: he lays hold of the best elements of the race to which he ministers, and trains and welds them into a force which he can use.[1]

Now here we at once observe that the training is intellectual training; that the 'best elements of the race' are said to be young scholars of higher intelligence than their fellows; that the object of the training is to create a force which the foreign missionary can use; and finally that all the early training of the race in native government of their family or tribe is set wholly on one side as of no account. The training given is essentially education in the narrow, modern, western sense of the word, a literary and intellectual training.

The bishop says that this is 'the only possible path of development'. It is not the only path; it is not even certain that it is the best path. That it is not the only possible path is proved by the history of the early church which certainly did not follow this path; for it was led from the beginning by 'elders': that it is not necessarily the best path may be doubted from his own description of it. In a country where all affairs of importance are weighed and decided by the elders, it is gravely open to doubt whether it is wise to begin by setting the elders on one side and training the very young to be the assistants of the foreign missionary. It is a contradiction of all the deepest and strongest convictions of the people: it dissociates church order at the very foundation from their natural conceptions of order. That the Church should begin by setting aside the elders in order to elevate the youngest to guide their elders is indeed to present to the people a conception of church order as something utterly strange and subversive of all natural order. But church order is not the enemy of the natural and instinctive, the almost universal, conviction that the elders should guide the younger generation. If then it were true that this was the only possible path of development in the missionary's work, it would be at once apparent that the missionary's work was work of a very strange and dangerous character; and wise men of experience, not only in Madagascar, but in England, would look askance at it. A work which admits no possibility of development except upon the subversion of all natural order is indeed a work open to grave doubts.

[1] *The East and the West*, April 1909, p. 164.

That the bishop wholly ignores the traditional training of the race for positions of authority also raises some doubt as to the wisdom of his plans; because that training has in the experience of many ages produced men in every race and tribe who naturally command the respect of their fellows. They are possessed of a large fund of traditional wisdom: they have been tried and tested again and again in questions of difficulty by their neighbours and kinsfolk and friends. They know their people, and are known by them with a profound intimacy. They know how to speak and how to maintain any custom which they hold of importance. As Christians they surely should be the missionary's chief supports. No, not at all, says Bishop King. The best elements of the race are young boys of quick wits. The one thing of importance is not experience, or weight, but a sharp intelligent mind which can quickly acquire new and strange information. To be able to learn arithmetic and geography and reading and writing, that is the ability which proves a boy to be worthy of a place among the best elements of his race. I wonder if this is certainly true. I wonder whether the fact that a foreign missionary can easily 'educate' a lad necessarily proves that boy the best instrument for the propagation of the gospel or for the establishment of the church.

But the training is 'to produce a force which the foreign missionary can use'. Here is revealed the secret. This is the only possible way to produce a force which the foreign missionary can use. The work to be done is 'his work', and must be done in his way. Any instrument that he cannot use is useless. The grave elders of the village cannot easily be moulded into a shape to fit his hand. They are no good. A child can be moulded to fit his hand, and to do exactly what he wants done. But is it good for the church?

(2) The education of the first boys completed, they become a group of teachers or catechists. They can read the Bible, conduct prayer, give simple catechetic lessons, preach simple mission sermons. . . . They will form a sort of a ring about him. Some will live near him and help in his central church and school; others will settle in the villages round about, and take services, build churches, work schools, and thus in due course the mission out-stations are created, daughter churches to the central church where the missionary more especially works. This is the second stage of the work, when the alien missionary . . . has formed a group of native workers depending more or less closely on himself.[1]

[1] *The East and the West*, April 1909, p. 165.

Here we must observe what Father Herbert Kelly calls 'the familiar absurdity of the lay reader. The man who may not celebrate, because he is too uneducated and has not passed examinations, is allowed to preach and minister to souls!'[1] We must notice also that the bishop speaks of out-stations guided by these lay readers as 'daughters churches', as if a congregation without ministers, without sacraments, was a 'church'. This is a theory of the Church unknown to the Bible, unknown to early Church History, unknown to any Catholic teaching: it is indeed the flat contradiction of them all. And finally we are told that the 'group of native workers thus formed depends more or less closely on the alien missionary'. Thus the practical training of these men at this stage is training in familiarity with 'a church accustomed to regard the Lord's supper as an occasional luxury', and in dependence on what Bishop King calls the 'alien missionary'.

(3) The third stage is the 'college'. . . . Some sort of college must be formed which will ensure a better education to new boys who give themselves to the work. All alike declare that they *must* have *better trained* men. In consequence some one missionary withdraws from pastoral and evangelistic work, and concentrates his efforts upon a college. The best existing native workers are called in to help him, and a much more thorough and effective training, lasting from three to five years, is given to those who have passed through the local mission schools. A determined effort is made to develop the spiritual life and mental powers of a few selected native boys. . . . These better trained men come out of college prepared to work as catechists of a superior sort.[2]

Here we must observe that it is the need of the missionaries for men better trained in their system which creates the demand for the college. The theory of preparation supported by Bishop King is beginning to show its weakness. The catechists half-trained at the earlier stage have been put into an impossible position to guide congregations of men of larger experience than their own, by the light of a smattering of western education and theology. They have been separated by their education from the people whom they are to teach. Too much responsibility for the conduct of the congregation has been thrown upon them. They have been half trained in a purely western and utterly strange manner of life. They do not know what

[1] *The East and the West*, Oct. 1916, p. 435.
[2] Bishop King's article, p. 165.

to do. They want to please their master, the foreign missionary, to whom they are solely responsible, they want to do things as he would do them; but they do not know how, and no one in the village can help them. They are isolated, cut off from their own people by their education, cut off from the foreigner whom they serve by race and habits of thought. Their one chance is to live precisely by his directions; but when he gives directions they very often cannot carry them out.

For instance, he wants accounts kept; and they cannot keep them well in his way; and the way of their fathers is not known or not approved by him, even if they had learnt, or could now learn, that way. So they get muddled. And this muddle enters into matters even more serious than accounts; and everybody is dissatisfied. The missionary naturally thinks that the fault lies in the lack of training: it never enters his head that he is beginning at the wrong end, and that he is putting the wrong man in the wrong place. The elders, if they were permitted, could manage all their local church affairs in their own way easily and successfully; but that would not suit the missionary's account book. And the work is 'his work', and must be done in his way. Consequently he cries aloud for better trained men.

And still the church is built on a lay foundation, with neither ministers nor sacraments, except as an occasional visit from the priest in charge of the district may permit. In all this training the idea of ministry is purely personal. Bishop King says that at this stage 'we are still some way from an ordained ministry—that is, men whose character and piety we can sufficiently trust and whose mind is adequately trained to allow us to present them for the gift of Holy Orders'.[1] This idea, that the gift of Holy Orders is a purely personal thing, is very dangerous. It is the church which has a ministry, not only an individual. If we allow ourselves to think of it as purely individual and personal we are in danger of falling, as we do fall, into serious mistakes. The minister exists, so to speak, apart from the church to which he ministers. He is given 'a charge', 'a cure of souls', 'a sphere of work', and so many souls are handed over to him. And thus the responsibility is all laid upon him, and the responsibility of the church is ignored. If ministers of Christ have a responsibility to Him for the care of the church over which He has made them overseers, the church also has a responsibility for the

[1] Bishop King's article, p. 166.

ministers; for in truth the ministry is given to the church, not the church to the ministry.

In appointing ministers for a congregation, it is as important to consider the needs of the church as it is to consider the character and the education of the individual; but by looking solely at the individual we forget the church. In the early Church we find local men ordained for the local church. They were ordained for that church; and they did not seek for some congenial sphere wherever they might see an opening or could obtain preferment. Thus the link between the church and the ministry was maintained. But in our system, when the ministry is considered a purely personal gift, men seek for themselves, or are sent by authority, to occupy this post or that, without any regard to the link which is thus snapped, and the consequence is that they often look upon 'churches' simply as places which offer them opportunities for the exercise of their gifts, or as steps in a ladder of preferment. But the link thus broken is not an unimportant one. In England, where the whole population moves from place to place with extreme ease and readiness, the evil is not so apparent; but in a country where generation after generation lives in the ancestral village, the link between the local church and its ministers is of great importance, and the importation of a stranger to act as minister to people whom he does not know intimately, and who do not know him and his whole family intimately, is a serious evil.

At this point the bishop goes out of his way to repeat a familiar argument by which we moderns contrive to repudiate the teaching of the Bible and the practice of St Paul.[1] He says that some non-episcopal missions have taken a

> perilous short cut towards ecclesiastical completeness which must be avoided at all costs. . . . They have followed blindly what they conceived to be the practice of St Paul and St Barnabas. . . . They have bidden each little group of Christian converts select a local man of good character, and have appointed him to administer Holy Baptism and the Lord's Supper in the congregation which has chosen him. . . . They have failed to understand that the first Christian churches were bits broken off the local synagogues, and that there were usually to be found among the earliest converts men who had been well trained in the faith, the morals and the devotional life of Judaism.[2]

[1] cf. *Missionary Methods: St Paul's or Ours?* Chapter 3 and *The Establishment of Indigenous Churches: a dialogue.*
[2] Bishop King's article, p. 166.

He says that:

> The system does not work so badly as might have been supposed: but
> when all allowances are made he (the foreign missionary) feels sadly
> conscious that he has let the reins of power pass from his hands, and can
> only advise and exhort where he ought to rule.

This argument sounds curiously in the mouth of a Christian
bishop. The apostolic practice was not peculiar to St Paul and St
Barnabas, for it was followed over very wide areas long after the
death of the apostles. There were great numbers of small churches
in the apostolic and sub-apostolic age in Asia Minor, Armenia,
North Africa, and elsewhere which were certainly not 'bits broken
off the local synagogue', and the names of their first bishops are
certainly not Jewish names.

It is strange that a Christian bishop should ascribe the stability
and growth of Christian churches more to the power of training in
the faith, the morals and the devotional life of Judaism than to the
power of the Holy Ghost and of the grace of Jesus Christ. What is
less strange, but is very significant, is the bishop's strong emphasis on
the duty of the missionary to rule, and his scorn of the weakness of
exhortation and advice. He has rejected the practice of St Paul, and
with it apparently the spirit of St Paul, who certainly relied, as all his
epistles proclaim, upon the power of exhortation and advice. He
certainly did not maintain his power to rule by refusing ordination,
and he certainly did not lose it by ordaining ministers.

(4) The bishop says:

> The fourth stage in the preparation of a native ministry can only come
> slowly. The clergy must be selected in due course out of the body of
> trained native catechists; occasionally and to meet an immediate need a
> man of very partial training, who has done long service, and whose
> character has been well proved, may be selected, but as a rule knowledge
> as well as character—education as well as godliness—are necessary in a
> ministry which is to command the respect of a native church.

With regard to the appointment of clergy he says:

> It should be clearly laid down that a church has no right to expect to
> have clergy of its own race in sufficient numbers until it can pay for their
> maintenance. It is gravely open to doubt if the clergy of any church can
> as a whole be trusted to put forth their best efforts if their success or non-
> success in no way affects their income.

Here, we must observe once more, the emphasis upon intellectual training, and the ignoring of the training in government and management of practical affairs which is derived from the direction of the family or the tribe, as well as of the spiritual authority and influence which is very often possessed in the highest degree by men whom the bishop certainly could not train to be catechists and certainly would not ordain as clergy. And further we cannot but notice that very strange emphasis on pay. Father Kelly has remarked that 'the poor are largely deprived of the sacraments because priests are so expensive'.[1]

For generations after the death of the Apostle there were no paid clergy in the Church. If St Paul and his successors had followed the scheme of Bishop King the Church in Europe would have known neither bishops nor sacraments.

(5) The last stage—the most difficult of all—is the development of a native episcopate. The bishop asks:

Is it sufficiently realized that a native episcopate must be trained, that, if a native bishop is to arise in a missionary church, the body of men— natives—from among whom he must arise must be created? It may be said that we may select the best of our own native parish priests. In that case we must see to it that our native clergy are, some of them, in a full sense parish priests: at present they are too often mere assistant curates to the English missionary, and are not developing self-dependence, administrative gifts, and power of government. Among other things a bishop must be a governor; and to find a governor, we must create a body of parish priests who are accustomed to govern. . . . It is better that they should make mistakes in ruling than that they should never learn to rule at all. We must not set apart just one or two marked men as bearers of responsibility; we must create a whole class[2] . . . But beyond all else, the 'idea' is needed that a native episcopate 'ought to be'. Ideas come first in order of time; they are realized in due season. . . . The very 'idea' that there can and ought to be such a thing is only now rising above our intellectual horizon; and until the idea of a native episcopate is made familiar to our clergy and laity in the mission field we shall get no further towards creating it. In principle we teach that God is 'no respecter of persons', and chooses whom He will as the recipients of His Grace of Orders; but in practice we seem to be saying to our people, 'God wants you all to be Christians—some few of you to be priests; but He only chooses white men as bishops'. Let us, then, foster the true idea, and the thing itself will come in due time.

[1] *The East and the West*, Oct. 1916, p. 435.
[2] Bishop King's article, p. 169.

Here indeed is a remarkable thing! The whole of the preceding training has been training of the native workers in obedience to the missionary governor. At every stage the natives have been under the direction of foreigners upon whom they have been taught to depend for guidance and support. At every stage the supremacy of the 'alien missionary' has been asserted: he has been told that he must rule: he has been practising the art of ruling his native helpers. Now, all of a sudden, the foreigner is rebuked for ruling, and the demand is made that the natives should be trained in self-dependence and power of government, even at the cost of mistakes. The whole idea of the preparation is transformed. But, as the bishop has discovered, that is not an easy change. Missionaries who have been encouraged to rule and direct native catechists and teachers, naturally rule and direct native deacons and priests. A Christian community which has learned from the very beginning that their ministers depend upon the foreigner for support and guidance are not prepared to support native priests. The boys who have been educated in mission schools and colleges under the government of foreigners have learned from the very beginning to rely upon their foreign director. In a moment all this is to be changed: they must learn to act for themselves and to exercise responsibility, without any support. The foreign bishop in his action can rely upon the support of the missionaries: the missionaries in taking action can rely upon the support of the bishop and their fellow missionaries. Upon whose support can a self-dependent native priest rely? He cannot rely upon his own people, because they have not learned to expect any self-dependent action on the part of natives in the church: he cannot rely upon the support of the foreign missionaries, unless he does precisely what they do, as they do it: he cannot rely upon the support of the foreign bishop, unless the bishop happens to approve of his action; and that is not certain, if the native priest really acts for himself. Self-dependence in his case means an isolated self-dependence, a dangerous self-dependence. He is a paid official, generally with a wife and family to support. An error in the eyes of the foreigners may bring him to ruin. How can he not depend upon them?

We all know that a sudden change in the education of a child, or of a society, is a very serious matter. It is the beginning which is the most important of all, for on it all the later stages ought to be built: a break, even a little change, upsets the whole course of the education. But here is a break of the most fundamental character. An education in dependence is to be transformed into an education in independence. No change could be more radical. And how that change is to be made Bishop King does not tell us. The simplest way, perhaps the only safe way, would be to go back to the beginning and start all over again.

That is not the only change. Here Bishop King perceives that it will not do to train only one or two, or a few individuals. A whole class must be created. Why? Why, because isolated self-dependence is dangerous to the church. Men are not naturally isolated self-dependent individuals: they need the support of their fellows. But that is exactly the principle which was violated in the selection of young catechists to stand alone over a congregation of their elders. He himself said 'some of them may give way under the stress of temptation and loneliness'. The loneliness of a catechist trained by foreigners in mission schools and sent to take charge of a village congregation, and the dangers of that position, are familiar to all who have any knowledge of the mission field, and indeed to any man possessed of the smallest imagination. But if the catechist is lonely and isolated in his village, the native priest is not less isolated and lonely in his parish. At the very top of the tree, the episcopate, the bishop sees the danger. But he ought properly to go back once more to the very beginning, and see that it is an error to put a youth in an isolated position as a catechist, with no support except that of his foreign master.

When Bishop King speaks of the importance of making the idea of a native episcopate familiar to a clergy and laity, since that idea is, in his view, the idea of a head governor over a great number of clergy, of an official who is Chief even of the foreign missionaries, he is treading on very dangerous ground. For if he is right in saying that the European missionaries can hardly submit to such a rule, and if it is true that the mission has so managed its business that they can with difficulty withdraw, then to make such an idea familiar to a native clergy and laity who are beginning to feel their powers for self-government growing, must create grave difficulties. That way lies strife for the supremacy. It is hardly to be expected that the native clergy and the bishop and the missionaries will all agree exactly as to the moment when the day of independence has dawned. Missionaries and officials of missionary societies and bishops are always talking of the day of independence, but it is generally as 'far-off' or as 'in some years to come', 'some day', but never 'today'. Natives educated in colleges generally think that it should come earlier than the missionaries think good; and then the struggle begins in earnest. That such a struggle is the inevitable consequence of the training which we have been discussing is quite certain. Already in many of our missions signs of its advent are appearing, and they would be still more apparent if it were not that the native Christians largely depend upon the pecuniary support of the mission and fear to sacrifice it.

Lord Morley, referring to the government of our colonies, has told us that Mr Gladstone:

> . . . was never weary of protesting against the fallacy of what is called 'preparing' these new communities for freedom, teaching a colony like an infant by slow degrees to walk, first putting it into long clothes, then into short clothes. A governing class was raised up for the purposes which the colony ought to fulfil itself. . . . Whilst waiting for the grant of free institutions they are condemned to hear all the miserable jargon about fitting them for the privileges thus conferred; while, in point of fact, every year and every month during which they are retained under the administration of a despotic government, renders them less fit for free institutions. 'Our error lay,' he said, 'in the attempting to hold the colonies by the mere exercise of power.'[1]

That is precisely what we are doing in our missions. That is precisely the fallacy which lies at the root of the scheme which Bishop King sets forth.

I have dealt thus at length with Bishop King's article, because it is the best expression that I can find of the theory most commonly held amongst us. In this theory the consecration of a bishop is 'the crown and final attainment of the true church of the country'. We invert the biblical order at every point. Baptism is made the crown and final attainment of an attempt by a hearer to learn the doctrine and to keep the law, instead of the beginning of a new life: the priest-hood is made the final attainment of a church which has grown sufficiently in wealth to be able to support an official paid according to a scale which we think befitting his dignity, instead of a necessary and essential part of the constitution of a church: the church of the country is composed of a large number of groups of Christians instead

---

[1] *Morley's Gladstone*, vol. 1, pp. 360, 361.

K

of a large number of churches: the bishop is the last step in a long and weary path by which a church is created out of churchless, priestless, and non-sacramental congregations.

It is not surprising that disasters should befall a church so organized. To take an instance at random:

The Kacharis were the original inhabitants of Assam. The Rev. S. Endle, who laboured forty years in Assam, opened up missionary work among them, and about 1,000 were brought into the Kingdom; churches and schools were built, and there was every prospect of a mass movement. Since Mr Endle died, about thirteen years ago, there has been no one who had known the Kachari language. The Christians have dwindled to 400; they are visited as often as possible, but have to be ministered to in the Assamese language which they very imperfectly understand.[1]

Or this: 'The bulk of the Christians of Banting (in the Diocese of Sarawak) have lapsed back into heathenism,' and the bishop who writes of it asks: 'Why is it?' and answers his question by saying that:

In the old days of twenty or thirty years ago there was always a European priest in charge of this station, which was considered to be a stronghold of Christian aggressive work ... but since these workers moved on elsewhere we have been unable to replace them by resident European workers and the inevitable has occurred. There are plenty of resident Manangs, or Dyak witch doctors, in the village, and the people have gradually come under their sway, and the result is obvious.[2]

Such stories, and they are not infrequent, are always used as an appeal for more missionaries. But in truth these disasters are the result not of the absence of white missionaries, but of the misuse of them as pastors and leaders of the native congregations. In the first instance which I quoted those Kacharis should not have been dependent on one foreign missionary, who knew their language, for the simple ordinances which Christ ordained for all His disciples, and the small remnant which survived should not have received its spiritual sustenance in a language which it did not understand. In the second instance the heathen had ministers of their own, while the Christians, on the withdrawal of the white missionary, had none. A Christian native bishop or priest ministering the sacraments to his

---

[1] *The East and the West*, Oct. 1920, p. 325.
[2] *Mission Field*, Dec. 1903, p. 279.

people would have been the equal of any Manang. Deprived of all sacraments, without any Christian ministry or organization, they fell. Is it surprising that when Christians are deprived of the means of grace they should fall? Christ did not ordain the sacraments as luxuries, but as the necessary means of grace. When we deprive His people of His Grace in order to maintain a type of ministry trained and paid in our peculiarly Western way, we cannot be surprised if disasters befall us and our converts. Yet there are men who would say that the risk of a moral failure such as that of the church at Corinth outweighs the lapse of whole congregations from the Christian Faith.

I said in my second chapter that the spontaneous expansion of the Church involved not merely the multiplication of Christians but the multiplication of churches. The spontaneous growth of the early Church depended not only upon the freedom with which its members did their duty and preached Christ wherever they went; it depended not less upon the freedom with which churches, real churches, with presbyter bishops or bishops and priests, were established. Then any church could, and did, provide for any new groups of converts by giving them an organization like its own.[1] Such expansion is impossible on the theory which we have been considering. It is impossible to imagine the spontaneous activity of an individual resulting in the creation of a new church. It can only result in the creation of a new congregation dependent upon the few priests in the country and adding to their already overwhelming burden. The church in the country cannot create a new church like itself: it must wait until sufficient money has been subscribed to endow a new bishopric. It is perfectly clear, then, that a theory such as we have been considering hinders to an inculculable extent, even if it does not absolutely prevent, any spontaneous expansion. But the moment that we think of churches in the apostolic sense of the word, we see at once that the spontaneous activity of individual members might speedily result in the multiplication of such churches all over the country.

There is another story. Father Herbert Kelly, in two articles in the *East and the West*[2] from which I have already quoted, set it forth. He proclaimed that we ought to return to the primitive system, exactly

[1] The fact that it early became a general custom that three or more bishops should unite in the consecration of a bishop does not affect the argument.
[2] April and October, 1916, pp. 182, 192, 429, 439.

that system which Bishop King called a 'perilous short cut', 'to be avoided at all costs'. Father Kelly says:[1]

Let us imagine ourselves in some small primitive church met to choose a pastor. Our course is quite obvious. Normally, we want an experienced, a middle-aged Christian of strong character and independent position, who is not, and need not be, afraid to speak to us, a man zealous for his faith and who understands it, learned in the Scriptures. We have no college-trained men among us, but at forty a man has learnt from life. We are not trying young experiments. We want someone to lead us and help us such as we are, and we all know one another's mind and capacities much better than a board of examiners will ever do. . . .

Thus the ministry was provided, but how was it provided for? We know that the early Church did not pay personal salaries, since the habit of doing so was made a charge against the Montanists. . . . If the pastor is sent the sender will be responsible. . . . If, however, the village chooses one of its own members no difficulty arises. He is sure to be a middle-aged man; he is already providing for himself, and is in a position to go on doing so, no doubt with some assistance of gifts in money, kind, or labour to compensate for any loss of time through his pastoral labours. . . .

The village farmer-priest is the father of a family. Of course, being a priest he is a priest in the Catholic Church, but this does not mean that he is free to accept a 'call' wherever sufficient inducement offers. He is ordained to his own people. . . .

I have dealt with the country ministry first, because the simplest condition brings up what is most fundamental. That the country ministry is to us the most difficult problem seems to show that we have somehow missed the fundamentals. The Church cannot exist without a ministry, but the ministry exists for the Church. That is a sufficient ministry which supplies what the Church really needs at the time. When the needs of the Church become more complex, the ministry will naturally be elaborated to meet them. Even in towns in the early stage, and in small towns for a long time, a local ministry on the village plan will suffice. . . .

In the cities, quite at the beginning, the system was the same as in the country, but the difference of circumstances produced a rapid development. The growing mass of church business gave rise to the minor orders of readers, acolytes, etc., and thus provided an opening for young men who might like to devote their life to the clerical profession. . . . In the towns the bishop was normally, though not necessarily, chosen from the professional clergy. This professionalism was not regarded as fundamental. It grew up where it was wanted, and the business which called it into being provided the means for its support.

[1] *The East and the West*, Oct. 1916, pp. 430, 431, 436.

Father Kelly differs from Bishop King in his estimate of the value of traditional training, he desires to see ordained the experienced middle-aged Christian of strong character and independent position. He realizes that among the first converts there are many such men, the depositaries of the immemorial wisdom of past generations. In every village, in every town there are such men, the natural leaders of their people. It is such men as these that he suggests should be the leaders of the infant church, its first priests and bishops. Bishop King, on the other hand, takes no account whatever of this traditional training.

Father Kelly differs from Bishop King in insisting that the Church must begin with the appointment of priests and bishops. He says that 'the Church cannot exist without a ministry'. He talks of the appointment of lay readers as an absurd fallacy, he speaks of 'the familiar absurdity of the lay-reader'. Bishop King on the other hand makes that 'familiar absurdity' the foundation of his whole scheme of preparation for a native episcopate, and calls congregations ministered to by young catechists churches.

Father Kelly differs from Bishop King in his estimate of the value of pay. Bishop King holds that 'it is gravely open to doubt if the clergy of any church can as a whole be trusted to put forth their best efforts if their success or non-success in no way affects their income'. Father Kelly says that 'a pecuniary interest in Christianity is not in itself a good, but a temptation'.

He differs also from Bishop King in his estimate of clerical training. Bishop King's whole system is based upon an intellectual training. Father Kelly says:

> College training constitutes a very serious danger. All professional training runs a risk of becoming too technical and abstract. Theological education is at the present more deeply involved in this evil than any other, and in nothing is the mischief so great. . . . I have heard a catechist address heathen villagers for an hour on the history of religious development. The ignorance of the village farmer-priest is no danger at all. The ignorance which is a danger is the pseudo-knowledge of a half-trained— or still more, of a very highly trained—professional agent, drawn to justify his everlasting sermons by the originality of patent Christianities picked up goodness knows where.

And curiously enough Bishop King, for all his emphasis on the training of the professional agent, closes his paper with a warning which would have been in place in Father Kelly's articles. 'We must take care,' he says, 'that our trained men do not lose in simplicity and directness of character what they gain in intellectual development.' A missionary in South Africa wrote somewhat as follows: 'I am staying with C., an untrained catechist of the old sort; he seems to get hold of the people in his own simple way; such men seem to me better evangelists than the trained men from our colleges.' That warning is sorely needed; for this comparison between the trained and the untrained catechist comes to us from many quarters. But nothing is more futile, though nothing is more common, than to imagine that we can avoid a danger by saying that we must avoid it, when it is inherent in our practice. It is like the action of an habitual drunkard who walks into a public house saying: 'I must avoid getting drunk.' So we say that we must avoid the danger of nursing our converts while we are busy arranging everything for them. So we say we must secure for our native priests full opportunities for learning independence whilst we pay them. And so here this evil is not to be amended by saying thatthe college authorities must take care to avoid it. Its roots lie in the fact that we have despised and set at nought the natural training of experience and have put in its place an artificial and intellectual training before the great body of the people was ready for it, and the inevitable consequence is that those who receive it are separated as by a great gulf from their people.

Father Kelly well says that the 'idea of a strictly local ministry, unprofessional, untrained, and unpaid, seems to us inconceivable, though we are very conscious of our own difficulties'; but he pleads 'that it is an error of judgment to assume that because we have now reached an exclusively professional system, therefore a professional system, with all its entanglements, ought to be forced on a quite new church'.

Objection is sometimes made to the consecration of native bishops on the ground that Bishop Crowther's episcopate was not an unqualified success; but we must not forget that the native episcopacy which Father Kelly proposes is not the episcopacy of which Bishop Crowther was a victim. Bishop Crowther was a native thrust into an impossible position. He was expected to take the place, and do the work, of a European bishop of the type with which we are familiar. He was the only bishop in a very large area set to direct and govern a large number of clergy and lay ministers who were not ready for a native bishop standing in an English bishop's shoes. There was no African Church in any real sense of the word. He was really an agent of the Church Missionary Society in Episcopal Orders. He was dependent upon the Society. As Bishop Melville Jones has said:

> The Niger Mission under his (Bishop Crowther's) regime was not a truly African Church. It was largely the accident of the deadly nature of the climate which led to the whole of the mission staff being of the negro race, and that was the only sense in which it was African. It was supported almost entirely by English contributions. There was little or no church organization which would lead to a system of self-government.[1]

Under such circumstances what wonder is it that men found in his episcopate cause for harsh criticisms! But that is not the sort of native episcopacy which St Paul established, or Father Kelly advocates. No objection to an apostolic practice can be founded on an instance which did not even remotely resemble the apostolic example.

It is interesting to observe that in matters such as we have been discussing in this chapter our adversaries sometimes see more clearly than we do ourselves. We are told, for instance, that in Madagascar:

> the formation of a native church and the growth of a native ministry is the one thing which France, as represented by her present administrators, most fears and dislikes. . . . They repudiate any intention of hindering the work of alien missionaries: such persons are evidently regarded as necessary evils in an imperfect world; and it would seem that they believe that the alien's work will produce results destined soon to pass away.[2]

These French administrators see that a church which depends upon alien bishops and priests must necessarily be weak, and that they can deal comparatively easily with European governors. They see also that the church cannot possibly extend widely or rapidly, or become a power among the natives, so long as the foreigners remain in authority. On the other hand they see that a native church fully organized and equipped with bishops and priests, would at once assume a more permanent and dangerous character. The church would have its roots in the island: it could grow and expand: it would be extremely difficult for them to uproot it: it

---

[1] *IRM*, April 1912, p. 252.
[2] Bishop King's article, p. 163.

appears doubtful whether they could ever check its advance by any regulations which they could make. Since the one thing which they dread is the revolutionary power of Christ's Gospel, they naturally look upon our hesitation and caution in ordaining priests, and our refusal to consecrate native bishops, with approval. They see that the ordination of native priests and still more the consecration of native bishops, and the establishment of native churches in the apostolic sense of the word, would at once open wide the door for spontaneous expansion. And it is spontaneous expansion that they fear, and rightly fear, if they do not wish to see the church established throughout the length and breadth of Madagascar.

Now when our enemies see, and tell us that they see, that a certain course of action would inevitably lead to a result which they dread but we earnestly desire, when they congratulate themsleves upon the fact that we do not take it, we surely might well learn the lesson which they teach. The spontaneous expansion of the Church is impossible or at any rate is severely checked by our refusal to recognize that the apostles knew how to organize the Church so that it could expand spontaneously and rapidly, and we are simply defeating our own ends and rejoicing the hearts of our enemies by refusing to recognize it.

CHAPTER 9

The Way of Spontaneous Expansion

The rapid and wide expansion of the Church in the early centuries was due in the first place mainly to the spontaneous activity of individuals. As I pointed out in my first chapter, a natural instinct to share with others a new-found joy, strengthened and enlightened by the divine Grace of Christ, the Saviour, inevitably tends to impel men to propagate the Gospel. The early Church recognized this natural instinct and this divine Grace, and gave free scope to it. Very many of the Christians in those local churches had no doubt become Christians, led by the spontaneous zeal of someone who was a Christian before them. The names of a few great apostles were known to the whole Church; but the first teachers of the majority of the Christians were probably unknown to any but those whom they had quietly influenced. No one, then, was surprised at the spontaneous efforts of individual Christians to convert others to their Faith. They probably thought it quite natural. Thus as men moved about there were constantly springing up new groups of Christians in different places.

The Church expanded simply by organizing these little groups as they were converted, handing on to them the organization which she had received from her first founders. It was itself a unity composed of a multitude of little churches any one of which could propagate itself, and consequently the reception of any new group of Christians was a very simple matter. By a simple act the new group was brought into the unity of the Church, and equipped, as its predecessors had been equipped, not only with all the spiritual power and authority necessary for its own life as an organized unit, but also with all the authority needed to repeat the same process whenever one of its members might convert men in any new village or town. Thus the results of the spontaneous labour of any individual Christian were naturally and easily consolidated and established within the unity of the Church.

L

143

I

This spontaneous activity of the individual, rooted as it is in a universal instinct, and in a Grace of the Holy Spirit given to all Christians, is not peculiar to any one age or race. We are familiar with it today. It constantly shows itself, and it would repeat the history of the early Church, if it were not that our fears have set up barriers in the way of its proper fruition, as I have attempted to show in earlier chapters. What we see today is the spontaneous zeal of Christians attempting to repeat, so far as they can, the early history of the Christian Church. The only reason why such spontaneous activity on the part of our converts has not resulted in the foundation of churches, is because our bishops have treated them in a very different way from that in which the bishops of the early centuries treated those who did precisely the same work. They equipped them and set them free; we have refused to equip them, and have bound them to the foreign organization of our mission. Thus we have cast down the men whose spontaneous zeal led them to convert their neighbours and friends by setting over them our trained and paid lay catechists; thus we have discouraged any others who might have followed their example. We have looked upon such spontaneous activity as something strange and wonderful. When we find an example of it told in our missionary magazines we generally find it associated with notes of exclamation and expressions of astonishment or anxiety. We have not known how to expect it, we have not known how to deal with it, and consequently it is not unnaturally more rare than it ought to be. Still it remains so essentially the natural action of that instinct to impart a joy, and that gift of the Holy Spirit who is the Spirit which desires and strives after the salvation of men, that in spite of our discouragement it constantly breaks out afresh. I have already had occasion to refer to some examples, I will here only cite two more as typical of a larger number.

(1) An African priest in charge of the mission at Tarquah on the Gold Coast gives the following account of one of his experiences:

I was called to visit some Christians at a village 163 miles from my station. . . . When I arrived I met about a hundred converts waiting for baptism. A young man from one of our stations, who has no teacher, had managed to learn to read a little of the New Testament and the Prayer Book in Fanti. He went up to this village, where some of his relations

144

lived, early in 1920. There he started teaching his own people, and the good news spread. They built a little church and for a year he laboured hard, teaching them as much as he could every morning before they went to their farms, and in the evening before they retired to rest. When he thought that they were ready for baptism, he heard of our scarcity of clergy and encouraged them to wait. After careful examination on my arrival I baptized forty-five adults.[1]

(2) Last month I had the Rev. Fong Hau Kong here for three weeks, to assist me by visiting some of my Chinese congregations. I sent him to Tuaran, about twenty-two miles from here, where there was a congregation that had never been visited by a clergyman since its settlement in the country. I had received an invitation to go to them, but I thought it better to send Mr Fong, as I have no knowledge of Chinese. He found a congregation of over forty Christians who had come from China nearly ten years ago, and settled as gardeners. They had elected as their teacher and reader one of their party, a man named Chang Shu Chung. He had in his early days been a teacher of a heathen school, but was converted to Christianity, and subsequently became a teacher in a mission school at Foo Chow. At first the community subscribed to pay a salary to their teacher, but later they were not so prosperous, and the salary ceased. Chang Shu Chung has, however, gone on with his work without any pay, and Sunday after Sunday has not failed to assemble the people for worship in the little church which they built for themselves. On the Sunday that Mr Fong spent with them he had a congregation of over forty, and administered Holy Communion to fourteen, and Baptism to one adult and eleven infants. This was the first occasion since they left China that they had been visited by a priest, or had an opportunity of receiving the sacraments.[2]

We see in both these cases a spontaneous expansion of the Church so far as these people were able: we see what might have been churches founded without any assistance, or direction, from the foreign missionaries. These people were self-supporting: they received no grants of any description from any society, they were able to supply all their own needs: they had built their own churches and they maintained their own services. Their leader was exercising what in an earlier age would have been called a charismatic ministry. They were self-governing, directing all the affairs of their own church. All that was needed for their establishment was that their leaders should have been ordained; for in both cases they had evidently been taught, or at any rate had somehow learned, that

[1] *World Wide Witness*, SPG Report for 1921, p. 84.
[2] *Borneo Miss. Chron.*, Aug. 1911.

only ordained men could baptize or administer the Lord's Supper. If this difficulty had been removed by Ordination, then in each case we should have seen at once the creation of a new church on truly apostolic lines, and the example so set would certainly have encouraged and inspired other native Christians to have followed the example set them.

Churches so founded would have been unquestionably native churches. The least intelligent native looking at them must at once have perceived that here was something which it needed no foreigner to maintain. They would have been native churches in a very different sense from those pseudo-national native churches which we talk about creating. Such churches would bring new life into the mission field, and open all the doors closed to us. The existence of one prophesies the conversion of the country. As I said before, these cases are not rare: almost every country in the world can show similar examples, and in some parts of the world they are quite common. The Bishop of Lagos, for instance, has told us that in Southern Nigeria the greatest progress of recent years has been due not so much to the direct work of the European missionaries, or of paid African teachers, as to the spontaneous work of untrained and unpaid native Christians.[1]

I believe the time is ripe for this advance. I have already tried to show that our present missions are not the natural homes of spontaneous expansion; but the societies themselves are doing something to prepare the way. They are now tending to concentrate more and more upon medical, educational and social work carried on in institutions; and as they do that, their resources in men and money will be so fully occupied that they must inevitably withdraw more and more from direct evangelistic work, and look upon this work as the proper work of native Christians; and many of our evangelistic missionaries are certainly looking in this direction. There is, therefore, a good hope that a movement towards spontaneous expansion may arrive at a propitious moment.

II

Let us suppose then that a missionary hears of such a case as one of those which I have quoted, or himself by his preaching has prepared a small body of men for baptism. Let us suppose that some of them

[1] CMS *Gleaner*, April 1921, p. 69.

have been baptized. We must realize that baptized Christians have rights. What are those rights? They have a right to live as Christians in an organized Christian Church where the sacraments of Christ are observed. They have a right to obey Christ's commands, and to receive His Grace. In other words they have a right to be properly organized with their own proper ministers. They have a right to be a church, and not a mere congregation. These are the inalienable rights of Christians, and we cannot baptize people and then deny their rights, or deprive them of them. When we baptize we take responsibility for seeing that those whom we baptize can so live in the church.

What then ought the missionary to do? If he has baptized the first converts we may take it for granted that he has assured himself that they are in the Faith, and he ought then to invite the bishop to act towards them as the apostles and their immediate followers acted in like case. The little group must be fully equipped with spiritual power and authority; and the bishop ought to deliver to them the Creed, the Gospel, the Sacraments and the Ministry by solemn and deliberate act. It is to do that work that we have missionary bishops.

(1) The bishop must deliver to them what St Paul called 'the tradition' (of which the Apostles' Creed is the later expression) that they may have a standard by which to try all that they may hear later. The Creed is a touchstone. It is by that that they will know whether any teaching they may hear is to be received or to be rejected. It does not follow that every member of that little church must know by heart a form of words as long as the Apostles' Creed; but it does follow that when each has heard it (and it may be expressed in very simple language so that the most ignorant can really *hear* it), he must be prepared to say, 'That I believe: That is my belief.' It is in this sense that the Creed is to be delivered to the church. Thereafter it is theirs. It belongs to them as much as it belongs to us.

(2) The bishop must deliver to them the Gospel, that they may know where to turn for instruction. For they must learn from the very beginning to rely upon God, not upon men, for spiritual progress; upon the Bible, not upon human teachers, for spiritual instruction. Here again, when he delivers the Bible to the church, it does not follow that every member in the congregation must be able to read it; but it does follow that all the Christians must learn

to revere it, and to know it. Consequently in such churches every possible mark of honour should be attached to the power to read and explain the Bible. Double honour to those who labour in the word and doctrine. The priest in such a church is not necessarily the preacher. The Bible is read by those best able to read it and expound it; but no man's mouth should be closed, and the most illiterate will sometimes be found able to make a comment of the most profound spiritual significance because it is rooted in his experience.

A writer is quoted in the *International Review of Missions* for October 1920,[1] as saying:

> A village panchayat may be an assembly of illiterate men, but it is not an assembly of ignorant men, by any means. Nor are they men uneducated in matters of government. Indian villagers, even pariah villages, have had centuries of education in matters of government and administration. It is often because our missionaries do not know enough of the vernacular really to follow an Indian palaver that they fail to discover how much sound sense and clear reasoning and practical wisdom there is in it.

And the same truth applies to the church. Illiterate members often bring to the church a profound spiritual knowledge, and a sense of the practical application of Christian truth to daily life, which is hidden from the accomplished student. This then is what I mean by the delivery of the Gospel to the church. The Bible is delivered to the whole Church as the message of God to the whole Church. Thenceforward it belongs to them and is in their care. It is theirs as much as it is ours.

(3) The sacraments must be delivered to the church. The bishop must make sure that they have learnt the manner and the meaning of their observance. They must be taught how to administer them, and how to receive them, practically. They must not be allowed to think, as some of them may have gathered from their observation of a mission station, that baptism is the end of a long probation during which a man has proved his capacity to observe Christian laws; but they must think of it as the beginning of a Christian life which a man cannot live without God's Grace. They must be taught how to administer it, and if necessary they must be warned of the grave dangers which may ensue if they abuse its use, dangers from which the whole congregation, and the whole Christian Church may suffer. They must be taught how to administer the Holy Communion, and how to re-

[1] p. 560.

ceive it, and that in a very practical way. They must be taught the meaning of the Holy Communion, and here I am very bold. I have a profound belief in the power of the sacraments. I believe that in a divine way the use of them teaches the teachable their inward meaning so that the Church grows by degrees into a deeper and deeper sense of the divine Grace imparted in them; and therefore I think that we need be in no hurry to attempt to teach new converts all that we think we know about them. I think it suffices if we begin with some one aspect of the Holy Communion, and that the one which our converts can most easily apprehend, whether the Common Meal at which Christ is the Host, or the Common Sacrifice which all offer together, or the Common Thanksgiving for the Common Salvation through the death of Christ. If they learn one of these in its simplest form, they can learn the others by degrees. Much they will learn without any teaching from others, by their reading of the Bible in common, much from participation; for in the common rite they will find in experience a common bond between Christian and Christian, and of all with Christ. And by degrees they will discover the profound significance of such Communion with one another and with Christ. Thus the first teaching need not be long or difficult of apprehension. This is what I mean by the delivery of the sacraments to the Church: they should be delivered to the Church as a whole; and the Church as a whole should be responsible for their proper observance. When the Corinthians misused the Lord's Supper, St Paul rebuked the whole Church.

(4) Ministers must be ordained that the church may have a Christian government and officers to direct the proper conduct of the church and the due administration of her rites.

The selection of these officers should not be difficult. St Paul in the pastoral epistles has laid down, very clearly, rules to guide a bishop in the selection of such officers. They were to be, he said, men of good moral character, free from the besetting vices of their people, men of experience and weight, men held in the highest respect by the members of the church and their heathen neighbours, men who knew the tradition and could uphold it, men who could maintain order by their moral superiority; in fact the men whom any decent society would naturally choose for its leaders. To these men must be delivered the authority to administer the sacraments and to guide and govern the church in its religious services and its daily social life. No question of pay should be raised or considered. St Paul did not raise it: we need not.

But here again it is the Church as a whole which receives officers, not officers which receive a Church. Ministers should be given to a church, not a church to a minister, and the Church as a whole should be responsible for the good conduct of its officers, just as the officers are responsible for the good conduct of the Church. When a member of the church at Corinth committed a moral offence St Paul did not rebuke the elders of the church only, he rebuked the Church as a whole. A church thus constituted is a real church in the apostolic sense of the word.

(5) There is one other point which I think the bishop should impress upon the church if he is seeking for spontaneous expansion. It is not that he should exhort them to take the Gospel to their neighbours; but that he should tell them what to do when they have made converts in their neighbourhood too remote to be intimately attached to their own body, or in case people from a neighbouring village came to them to learn the Christian Faith. He should tell them first to make sure that the new converts are really converts to the faith of Christ and understand the *use* of the Creed, the Gospels, the Sacraments and the Ministry, and then to send word to the bishop.

III

Having done this the missionary and the bishop should leave that newly constituted church to find out for itself what being a church means in daily practice, to find out that it can do things as a church. When I say that he must leave such a church to find out for itself what a church is, I do not mean that he should neglect it; for he ought to take thought for its education. We must learn the distinction between leaving Christians to learn what they can only learn for themselves, and abandoning them. It is a distinction which we find it hard to make; it is a lesson which we find it hard to learn. The moment any one suggests leaving new converts to find out for themselves by their experience without the guidance of a foreign missionary how to manage the simple affairs of a simple village church, instantly the father-mother, elder-brother, directing, spirit of the energetic missionary rises in revolt and cries: 'You cannot abandon them so early to their own devices.' To leave new-born churches to learn by experience is apostolic, to abandon them is not apostolic: to watch over them is apostolic, to be always nursing them is not apostolic: to guide their education is apostolic, to provide it for them is not apostolic. The missionary and the bishop must watch over their education.

Instantly we perceive that the education of which we are speaking is something very different from what is commonly called missionary education. Missionary education, commonly so called, is a thing of schools and colleges, and for the few. The education of which we are now speaking is the education of the church and embraces the whole Christian community. The education of which we are speaking is education in the church, of the church and by the church.

It is essentially religious education, not in the sense in which we talk of religious education in schools where religious education means instruction in the subject-matter of the religion, given by a teacher for an hour in a day which is devoted mainly to secular education, but in a very different sense. This is an eductaion in the management and direction of the Christian church as a body, and of the family as a Christian family. The religious life is the one subject, and there is no other. The one thing to be learned is how to live the Christian life in that state and social order in which the Christians find themselves.

It is an education which Europeans cannot conduct because few, if any, Europeans can ever really understand the position of new converts from heathenism: they cannot look at the position from the inside; and it can only be the fruit of an internal growth. But if they cannot conduct it, they can watch over it, and they can assist it, as well as retard it. The education of the church is rather to be compared to the education of an infant in the use of its faculties than to the education of a boy in the Latin grammar. A good master can teach a boy Latin grammar. It is in a very different sense that a mother teaches a child to walk, or to see and to observe. Nature will teach the majority of children to walk, if they are allowed the use of their limbs. So the church learns the use of its faculties if it is allowed the use of its faculties.

The man then who would guide such a church as I have described and assist its education must obviously get out of the way to give it room; because if he stays, or if he leaves some one from outside in charge, it will plainly not have room to move. But he must watch over it and warn it by instruction when it is in danger of going seriously astray, or of falling heavily. The exact point at which such warning is necessary is a question of the most intimate delicacy; and it can only be solved by the instinct and insight of the educator with the watchful eye. It is impossible for any one else to judge, or to lay down any rule beforehand.

This practical education of the church I have put first, because it is the most important and the most fundamental education. The church must learn to use its faculties, and it can only do that by using them.

In doing this it will by itself both reveal and train the leaders of the future. By exercising government in the small body, the real leaders of the church learn to govern and direct a church composed of many such little churches. By teaching in the small body they learn to instruct a church composed of many such churches. By active evangelistic work in their own neighbourhood they learn to lead a mission in a whole province.

I said that the education was wholly religious. It is an education in how to apply the Christian faith to life under the conditions in which the Christians live. That is the one thing which matters, and that cannot be learnt in a school, but only in the world of life. Nevertheless there are certain aids which do materially assist the student of that art. I said that the one thing needful was to learn to apply the Christian Faith to life, and obviously to that end the study of the Bible is all important. When I spoke of the church, I took it for granted that at least one member of the congregation could read the Bible, and that there was a Bible or at least a Gospel in their language. That is not perhaps absolutely necessary; for the tradition might be handed down orally, and a church might make immense progress though all its members were illiterate. Nevertheless it is obvious that knowledge of the Bible is of great importance. Generally speaking it is true that most of those earnest Christians who have spontaneously taught their friends and neighbours have received some instruction, and have learnt to read, and can, therefore, teach someone else to read. But if we suppose an absolutely illiterate community we should all agree that a man watchful of the education of the churches would desire that they should be able to have the Bible read to them, and would take steps to secure this as far as he could.

There are two ways in which that can be done; for I exclude of course the sending of a paid mission teacher to live in the place and to do for the church everything that it ought to do for itself. The church can either invite someone who is able to read to teach a few of its own members to read, or it can send one or two of its members, or some of its members can go of their own free motion, to learn this art elsewhere. Neither of these courses is difficult, provided that the Christians have learned what is the place of the Bible in the church. If they have learned to pay it due honour they will respect and admire those who have knowledge of it, and out of it can show them larger and truer conceptions of Christian doctrine. There is no need to insist upon this. Muslims travel from Nigeria to Cairo to learn the Koran. Men universally respect the man who possesses in larger measure than they do themselves knowledge of a subject which they feel to be of vital importance; and no one need have any anxiety that this rule will not apply.

From the point of view of spontaneous expansion, we have no need to think of secular education, as we call it, at all, nor to make any provision for it. It is quite certain that men who learned to read religiously for a strictly religious purpose would certainly in some cases begin to desire and to win for themselves and their children further education in what we call secular subjects. If there were no mission schools, they would still do it, by using government schools if there were any such; and if there were none they would in time create schools for themselves. Given any opportunity at all, it is quite certain that intellectual enlightenment would increase in a church which was the home of religious teaching. And such enlightenment beginning in spiritual illumination would be well founded, and the church would remain always a fountain of enlightenment. The whole church would grow together in enlightenment, as each member brought in a new contribution, and each generation made some advance.

To us progress might seem slow; but all true educationalists know well the importance of slow growth for solid progress, even in the education of the individual; and when we are dealing with the education of a community we are thinking in terms not of years but of generations, and we must learn not to despise slow growth. The one thing of importance is that there should be some growth, some progress, however slight it may be in the eyes of the casual observer.

This then is what I mean by watching over the education of the church. To some minds this may seem inadequate, and they may think that we should make better progress by exercising direct control and forcing the pace. But I hope I have given reason to think that this is not really true, when we consider that we are building for the centuries; and at any rate I hope that no one will now accuse me of advocating the abandonment of our converts to their own devices; for surely all that I have been saying is the direct opposite of abandonment. To watch and to assist spontaneous progress is certainly not to abandon converts to their own devices.

IV

The question may be asked; for it is nearly always the first question asked when any reform is proposed: How would you apply that to congregations which have learned from the very beginning to rely upon foreign support and guidance? Now it is plain that to ordain simple unpaid villagers and to constitute a church among them is quite a different thing from ordaining paid and trained mission agents. There may be, there are, among these paid agents men who, because they really have become the trusted leaders of their people, would continue to lead them, if they and the people whom they lead were free; but in many cases, if the people were free to choose, and the paid catechists had not the support of the foreigners behind them, the leaders whom we set to lead would not lead for another day. If we removed the pay and the support of our authority, the Christians would revert tomorrow to the guidance of their old and experienced fathers, and leave these trained native agents on one side. With such material it is impossible to constitute the church. It is a sad thing, but it is nevertheless true, that if we talk of establishing the local church, the very men who have trained leaders for the native church, cry out that those men whom they have trained are not fit for this purpose. Neither these foreign teachers nor these native teachers, nor the congregations led and directed by them are prepared. Here and there the bishop might find cases in which it would be possible to constitute the church at once; and perhaps those cases are really more numerous than I imagine. But however that may be, I myself look for the salvation of these pauperized communities rather through the influence which the sight of young churches advancing spontaneously in the freedom of the Gospel will exercise upon them than by any direct action or exhortation on our part; because I am sure that properly constituted churches would expand as they felt and knew their power.

The way to convert the older missions is to show them what spontaneous expansion means in practice. As I have said spontaneous expansion is spontaneous. It is not created by exhortation. It springs up unbidden. Where men see it they covet it, and when the converts of the older missions see it they will begin to desire it. Desiring it, they will begin to seek it, and in seeking it to express it. Meanwhile they continue as they are. The missionary of spontaneous expansion need not be over-anxious about them. He need not hasten to convert them. He can leave them to their present foreign leaders with perfect confidence, assured that they too will awaken when the time is ripe.[1] He will not lack room for his work because of their existence, for they never have, and never will, occupy all the land.

v

But some one may say:

> The expansion of the early Church was, according to your own statement, due in large measure to the fact that in the early church bishops were consecrated for the new churches who could in their turn consecrate others for any new churches which might spring up in their neighbourhood; but you asked for no more than the ordination of priests in the village churches, and they could not ordain priests for churches which might spring up in their neighbourhood. If you want to return to the practice of the early Church, why do you not have the courage of your opinions, and ask that bishops should be again consecrated for the village, and town, churches; so that they might be able to propagate their like? If you did that, you would be consistent, and the native spontaneous expansion which you desire would become possible; but by your hesitation, though you establish indeed village churches, yet you leave those churches unequipped to propagate themselves unless they can obtain the assistance of a bishop who is probably a foreigner.

What answer can I give to that? I am, indeed, sure that to consecrate native village bishops is the true way of expansion. I believe that it would be far safer for the present Bishop of Honan or S. Rhodesia, for instance, to establish a hundred, or two hundred,

[1] In the only case in which I have heard of anything like what I have suggested in this chapter being done, I was told that this actually happened.

unpaid native bishops, not assistant bishops, but diocesan bishops ruling over small dioceses consisting of a village or a group of villages, because in ruling such dioceses men would learn the meaning of episcopal authority in its simplest form, and so be prepared to occupy the position of metropolitans as the churches grew in numbers; but if, as Father Kelly said, the idea of a strictly local ministry, unprofessional, untrained and unpaid, seems to be inconceivable, much more does the idea of a local episcopate, unprofessional, untrained and unpaid, seem inconceivable. It is possible that a bishop might be found to ordain local, unpaid, presbyters: that bishops should be found to consecrate local unpaid bishops seems incredible. I may deplore it; but so it is. To ordain only presbyters for the local churches would not be the best, nor the wisest, nor the safest course; but it would be something. It would be a move in the right direction, and it would, I believe, prepare the way for a native episcopate.

VI

The spontaneous expansion of the Church reduced to its elements is a very simple thing. It asks for no elaborate organization, no large finances, no great numbers of paid missionaries. In its beginning it may be the work of one man, and that a man neither learned in the things of this world, nor rich in the wealth of this world. The organization of a little church on the apostolic model is also extremely simple, and the most illiterate converts can use it, and the poorest are sufficiently wealthy to maintain it. Only as it grows and spreads through large provinces and countries do any complex questions arise, and they arise only as a church composed of many little churches is able to produce leaders prepared to handle them by experience learned in the smaller things. There is no need at the beginning to talk of preparing leaders to face great national issues. By the time the issues have become great and complex the leaders of the little churches of today will have learned their lesson, as they cannot possibly be taught it beforehand.

No one, then, who feels within himself the call of Christ to embark on such a path as this need say, I am too ignorant, I am too inexperienced, I have too little influence, or I have not sufficient resources. The first apostles of Christ were in the eyes of the world 'unlearned and ignorant' men: it was not until the Church had endured a persecution and had grown largely in numbers that Christ called a learned man to be His apostle. The missionaries who spread the Gospel and established the Church throughout the lands round the Mediterranean are not known to us as men of great learning or ability. Most of them are not known by name at all. Only when the Church had been established and had spread widely did Christ call the great doctors whose names are familiar to us by their writings, or by their great powers of organization and government.

What is necessary is faith. What is needed is the kind of faith which, uniting a man to Christ, sets him on fire. Such a man can believe that others finding Christ will be set on fire also. Such a man can see that there is no need of money to fill a continent with the knowledge of Christ. Such a man can see that all that is required to consolidate and establish that expansion is the simple application of the simple organization of the Church. It is to men who know that faith, who see that vision, that I appeal. Let them judge what I have written.

THE END

Index of Bible References